THE
PRO-ACHIEVEMENT
PRINCIPLE

Cultivate Personal Skills
for Effective Teams

Dr. Deb Bright

The Bright Press

HOW TO USE THIS BOOK

This book is intended to be read as both a learning and a coaching guide for cultivating skills for leaders and team members. Top among these skills are attitudinal alignment and a collaborative mindset. The book is formatted as a companion manual for advancing a spirit of positive and forward cooperation among individual team members. The steps, therefore, are sequenced as "Lessons" rather than chapters. End-of-lesson "Takeaways" are provided as teaching points for one-on-one or small group meetings, or as a quick reference for review purposes.

Bulk discounts available. For details email:
pdonnelly@brightent.com
Or contact special sales at 520 620-3500
View all The Bright Press titles and services at
www.drdebbright.com

Library of Congress Cataloging-in-Publications Data
Bright, Deborah
THE PRO-ACHIEVEMENT PRINCIPLE: Cultivate Personal Skills for Effective Teams
ISBN 978-1-7342060-0-5 (print) ISBN 978-1-7342060-1-2 (ebook)
ISBN 978-1-7342060-2 (Accompanying Workbook)

1. BUS106000 2. BUS071000 3. SEL027000

To view all books, BIZLETS, blogs, and articles published by
The Bright Press go to: www.drdebbright.com

The Bright Press
Attn: Permissions Advisor
756 S Tohono Ridge Place
Tucson, Arizona 85745
E-mail - pdonnelly@brightent.com

DEDICATION

This book is dedicated to the vast number of first responders as well as public servants who dutifully put themselves in harms way in their service to the public at large. Be they police, firemen, those in military service, healthcare workers, or any occupation requiring selfless dedication to the safety of citizens, this book includes them in the term "PRO-ACHIEVERS".

For these are people who embody the true meaning of the word *responsibleness* which is a term we use to describe a state of being in one's character. And it is that state of being that puts such Pro-Achievers way ahead of everybody when it comes to reliability, trust, honesty, politeness, and willingness to go the extra mile in the way they serve. They are the adults among us who take on the tasks so few of us volunteer to tackle.

DSB

CONTENTS

FOREWORD

In the spring of 2019 MIT Sloan Management Review and the Cognizant U.S. Foundation surveyed 4,394 global leaders, conducted twenty-seven executive interviews, and facilitated focus-group exchanges with next-gen emerging leaders worldwide to explore what the future of work portends for the future of leadership.

In brief, what this study concluded is that "A generation of leaders in large companies are out of sync, out of tune, and out of touch with their workforces, markets and competitive landscapes." Details of the study show that just 12% of respondents strongly agree that their leaders have the right mindsets to lead them forward. Additionally, only 40% agree that their companies are building robust leadership pipelines to tackle the demands of the digital economy.

On the other hand, the study identified several leadership teams that are embracing new and more effective ways of working and leading. The study notes that:

"The great leadership teams pay attention to cultivating not only the leader competencies and skill sets … but, also the mindsets required to build authentic and passionate communities of leaders. These teams don't simply rearrange the relationship between leaders and followers, they unleash the talents of every person to cultivate communities of leaders."

In an interview, Amber McCord of Johnson & Johnson expressed today's demands of leadership well when she said, "Organizations need to completely rethink what they are about and what it means to lead. It's not about one person or even those only at the top. In today's world everyone has to be a leader. We have to think of ourselves as members of a leadership community. It's not just something we talk about. It's who we are."

What Deb Bright tackles with *The Pro-Achievement Principle* is much more than changing unproductive behaviors for the advancement of achieving goals. She emphasizes the importance of collaborating in creative ways for all in the workforce—leaders, followers, and team members—to focus on adding value in everything they do. Her concept of "Pro-Achievement" is in complete harmony with the findings of the recent MIT/Cognizant Study's co-author and head of talent management and leadership at Cognizant, Carol Cohen, who said, "A key to success is artfully introducing new leadership approaches that particularly appeal to a new generation of employees while at the same time honoring the time-tested behaviors and attributes that inspire trust, build a sense of community, and motivate employees to improve performance."

This is a book that will help teams, and the individuals who make them up, achieve the expectations they collectively desire. In a profound and simple way, readers will learn how to deal with issues central to the challenge of advancing positive change in the behaviors of individuals, teams, and organizations in general.

This empowering, quick read is something you can do on your own, without help from a therapist, coach, or boss. Deb even includes lessons on how to spread the idea of The Pro-Achievement Principle up and down the organization by harnessing ideas generated by staff people at all levels. *The Pro-Achievement Principle* is more than another book on how to get commitment from workers. It stands as a short, highly readable manual for creating enthusiasm for going from good to better and from better to best. It moves the readers to take a close look inside themselves and examine ways that can make a "better me."

I have known Deb for a number of years now and she has made it her mission to seek practical ways to help people perform at their best. In this book she emphasizes, with the use of enlightening examples, how to look inside yourself to not only perform at high levels but to create true value for yourself, your team, and your organization.

Life is good,
Marshall Goldsmith
Spring 2020

This book is the first in a series known as THE PRO-ACHIEVEMENT SERIES to be published by The Bright Press. We call the books in this series *BIZLET*™**s,** which is a term invented by The Bright Press to describe a book that can be conveniently read in the time it takes to fly from Chicago to New York City. *The Pro-Achievement Principle* is designed to be a user's guide on how to become, and influence others to become, a Pro-Achiever. Broken down into quick lessons, you can start at the beginning and read straight through or pick it up and read a lesson or two when you have the time. To get an idea of what other **BIZLETs** will be forthcoming in the series, visit our website at:

www.drdebbright.com

ACKNOWLEDGEMENTS

We are particularly appreciative of three very talented freelancers who helped in the early development of this work. They are Frank Blackwell who assisted in the role of the book's developmental editor, and Wayne Purdin and George Mason who copyedited and formatted the material. Each of these talented editors provided contributions that were key in helping this book be the quality read that it is.

Working with the very talented people at the Nonfiction Authors Association (NFAA) has been a welcome and delightful experience. Stephanie Chandler and her team of energetic and competent editors, designers, and developmental experts are highly recommended for any author—both new and seasoned—who wants guidance through the publishing process while maintaining control of their work.

We are also grateful for the contributions and advice of our early reviewers. In particular, Natalie Edwards, president of The Network Doctor, offered valuable advice to make this book more understandable.

Lastly, we are honored by the willingness and enthusiasm of Marshall Goldsmith for his generous contribution of writing the foreword to the book. Marshall's signature phrase "Life is good" not only permeates his written works but is evident in his general outlook as well. Thank you, Marshall.

And most importantly, to my beloved husband Paul Donnelly, whose creative ideas helped to successfully drive this project. At every turn, he Pro-Achieved!

LESSON 1

PRO-ACHIEVEMENT: THE INDIVIDUAL'S TOOL FOR ORGANIZATIONAL SUCCESS

Can you name even one manager, team leader, supervisor, or CEO who would hesitate for a minute to accept an opportunity to get more and better-quality work from their employees, without having to offer monetized incentives like salary increases or bonuses? The lessons you will read in this BIZLET are specifically designed to show you the pathway to precisely that objective.

As a boss, team leader, project manager, business owner, or executive, you know all too well what kind of performance you would like from your direct reports and teams. But can you get it? Can they give it?

You bet you can, and they can too! And it's much easier than you might think.

How often have you asked in a state of frustration, "What do I have to do to get these employees to be more helpful to our customers?" or "Why don't my people pay more attention to what they're doing instead of thoughtlessly going through the motions?" or "Why don't they take more initiative?"

Research has shown that when these questions are asked, the people being talked about are quite likely unaware what level of performance is expected from them. But explaining specific expectations of performance to people is merely a starting point; it is far from empowering them to actually live up to those expectations. The real challenge is getting people to willingly commit to raising their own performance bar. Once that glorious moment happens, both of you will soon see results that will surprise you, them, and those with whom they work!

The contents of this BIZLET will detail, in simple terms, how you can help create an atmosphere brimming with employees and coworkers who step up and operate with a renewed sense of pride and enthusiasm in a way that echoes the motto, "If it's to be, count on me."

Does this sound like pie-in-the-sky thinking? Well, it's *not*.

EVERYONE WANTS TO BE PART OF A WINNING TEAM

What motivates working people today is the feeling of *belonging* and knowing that they're contributing something of value to the organization. They want to know how they can make a positive and valuable difference. It has to do with them feeling engaged in what they're doing. Think about it. Did you ever meet a young Marine who didn't exude pride in just being a Marine? Marines aren't the only ones with a desire to embody *Semper Fi*. Everyone wants to feel pride and commitment in what they do.

Everyone desires to learn and grow, both personally and professionally, during their career. Most relish the idea that if they didn't show up for work today, they'd be sorely missed.

People who are proud of what they do and where they work can always be found in workplaces that foster an atmosphere where individual achievement is promoted and valued as a key priority. Creating what's known as "an achieving atmosphere" involves making sure employees are properly equipped with essential attributes that are well within their control.

One of these key attributes involves *attitude*. But precisely what type of attitude is required for creating an achieving atmosphere? The pages that follow touch on many common types of attitudes. For example, you'll learn that the long-cherished "positive attitude" isn't enough, because its real meaning is vague and subject to misinterpretation. We're not simply talking about cheerleaders here.

"But," you might ask, "if not a positive attitude, then what?" You'll learn that the kind of attitude most compatible with an achieving atmosphere incorporates aspects of self-reliance, self-confidence, and yes, positive thinking. The culmination of such incorporated aspects is what some frequently call a "can-do" attitude. This term still isn't quite accurate, as "can-do" attitudes don't always foster a desire to make *a valuable difference* through one's actions as an individual or as a member of a team. In the lessons ahead, you'll discover and understand how to promote the kind of attitude set among workers that's the cornerstone for creating an achieving atmosphere among all people in any organization. The attitude a person has when going about what they do doesn't come about naturally; it's heavily influenced by the work environment itself. Teaching people to understand and adopt an "achieving attitude" and having it catch on like wildfire in your team is the core mission behind this BIZLET.

At this point you might be saying to yourself, "Wait a minute, this book is for leaders. I'm not yet anyone's boss or the head of anything! Why should I keep reading?" If so, take a minute to step back and ask yourself how you think leaders get to be leaders. Consider this: Leaders are not made by the appointment of others or by way of designated titles or signs on a desk. People become leaders from the inside out, not the outside in. Potential leaders must first grasp a true understanding of exactly what they can and cannot control.

Though you may not have the title of leader yet, we guarantee that what you learn here will kick-start the passion of the leader inside you, even if you don't yet think of yourself as a leader. And even if leadership is not your cherished goal, we promise that you will become a great team player after adopting the ingredients of Pro-Achievement.

Also, even if you are not yet in a formal leadership position in your organization, do not skip what is offered in Lesson 5 Recruiting Pro-Achievers: A Team Leader's Guide. When job openings come up in the organization where you work, what you read in Lesson 5 will give you a leg up on everyone you might find yourself competing with.

~

DO YOU THINK LIKE A PRO-ACHIEVER?

Print out and complete this self-scoring questionnaire to see how much you and your team think like pro-achievers. It's a great way for starting yourself and the team off to becoming the pro-achievers you all want to be.

GO TO: www.drdebbright.com/pro-achievement-bonus-page

LESSON 2

RESPONSIBLENESS: A CORE COMPONENT OF PERSONAL ACHIEVEMENT

Can you identify the hidden problem in the following dialogue between a boss and her direct report?

Boss: "Where's the Hutchinson report that was due two hours ago?"

Direct Report: "I'm sorry. I couldn't get it done on time because Joey in the legal department didn't give me the information I requested."

Boss: "Did you contact him?"

Direct Report: "I emailed him about an hour ago, but I still haven't heard from him."

Boss: "Why didn't you contact him sooner? And couldn't you just have walked over to his office and talked to him? His office is on your floor."
Direct Report: "Well, I guess I could have!"

If ever you find yourself in a conversation such as the one above, be aware that you're conversing with a person who has little understanding of what they can or cannot control.

The challenge the boss has in this brief scenario is a much broader problem than it appears. Getting her direct report to recognize span of control is the looming challenge she needs to tackle. The direct report in this scene recognized the responsibility he had, but he was missing the necessary ingredient of "responsibleness."

DIFFERENTIATING RESPONSIBILITY FROM RESPONSIBLENESS

Few people understand the true definitional difference between responsibility and responsibleness. No wonder. Responsibleness is a word that's rarely used; even the spell-check on my computer fails to recognize the word, despite its appearance in the *Oxford American Dictionary and Thesaurus*.

Having responsibility is often used to mean a level of importance someone has, a particular role they play, or something they're in charge of. We have a pretty good idea of what's meant when we hear that someone exhibits a sense of "personal responsibility." It's more than having responsibility for something: It has to do with one's character and dependability. It also implies trustworthiness that breeds confidence in relationships.

However, some people consider having personal responsibility more akin to a temporary obligation than to a kind of existential state of being. To give emphasis, clarity, and differentiation to this important character trait, in this BIZLET we've chosen to use the phrase *personal responsibleness*. Personal responsibleness, in contrast to personal responsibility, more accurately implies that state of being in a person's character—an ingrained quality, rather than situational behavior. It describes a competency and trustworthiness that we associate with those displaying a highly recognizable degree of reliability. People who have personal responsibility either take it on by choice or have it thrust upon them by circumstance. It often regards something they're in charge of, as in, "She is personally responsible for the XYZ department."

People who have personal responsibleness care about their tasks because they take ownership of them and invest their time and energy in them. They make sure that what they can bring to a task suits their own desired result. Specifically, they set their own high standards in completing tasks and do whatever is within their control to ensure that expectations are met or exceeded. To better clarify what distinguishes responsibleness from responsibility, consider the following real-life experience reported by a customer of Morton's The Steakhouse in Palm Springs, California. It exemplifies personal responsibleness in action.

During their visit to Palm Springs, a couple named Inez and Albert chose Morton's to celebrate their thirtieth wedding anniversary. There are many steakhouses in and around Palm Springs that the couple could have chosen for their anniversary dinner, but Morton's was near where they were staying and had prices well within their budget.

After being escorted to their table by the maître d', the couple ordered from their waiter, Chico, a medium-priced French Bordeaux to accompany their shared prime rib. Chico seconded their selection as "a good-quality wine." Returning to their table with the wine selection and learning that it was the couple's anniversary, Chico congratulated them and, with ceremonial panache, opened the bottle and poured a sample of the wine for Inez to taste. After taking a couple of sips, Inez hesitated slightly before cautiously announcing to the waiter and Albert that the wine had a "distinct vinegary aftertaste." Without any fuss,

Chico acknowledged her comments and removed the wine bottle from the table.

Within a short time, Chico returned to the table to inform the couple that the bottle he had served was the last of its kind in the cellar and presented them with another bottle he recommended as a similar vintage. Chico announced that the new bottle was slightly more expensive but quickly assured the celebrating couple that they were to enjoy the wine and not be concerned with paying any additional cost. Once into their meal, the couple received a visit from the restaurant manager who inquired about their satisfaction with the meal, the wine, and the service. Inez responded by saying, "Everything is top-notch. We haven't had to ask for a thing."

While they enjoyed their tasty entrée, Chico brought to the table a sample of the restaurant's newest side dish of sautéed mushrooms, which the happy couple enjoyed and then ordered. Following their meal, both the manager and Chico escorted Inez and Albert to the front of the restaurant, thanking them for their patronage.

Two days later, the couple received a call from the manager asking if everything was satisfactory and if there was anything they might have done differently to enhance their dining experience. As the manager expected, they told him they couldn't have dreamed of a more enjoyable evening and that they planned to recount the experience to their many friends.

Now turn the page on the above experience and picture yourself shopping at your local grocery store and being frustrated, unable to find that bottle of anchovies you specifically went there to buy. You spot a stock person walking by and quickly ask them where you might find anchovies. Rather than simply pointing you in the direction of aisle eight, the stock person personally escorts you to the exact location of an array of canned and bottled anchovies and then points out some that are on sale. The employee makes sure the item you select is the one you need before moving on.

These simple, everyday examples illustrate the way in which the manager, the waiter, and the grocery store employee approached their responsibilities. Each went a step further than what would normally be expected to satisfy their customer. They exhibited personal responsibleness while doing their job. They routinely understood and accepted what control they had over the execution of their job and used that control to the fullest extent. Sure, their actions may have been instilled by their managers' desire to deliver excellence in customer service, which is all well and good. However, wherever, and whenever each had been made aware of the control that was theirs to exert, it stuck, and the work ethic that ensued worked well for each of them. Personal responsibleness isn't a set of behaviors directed by others. Nor does it get its direction from a system of rules. Rather, it's the driving force behind a person's self-imposed standards of behavior.

Individuals don't have personal responsibleness because of what they do. Individuals do what they do because they have personal responsibleness. They operate with the belief that it's up to them to make things happen, unless circumstances beyond their control make that outcome impossible.

It doesn't take long to recognize people with personal responsibleness. They're the auto repair person who tightens your wheel bolts, safety checks your tire pressure, and recommends you change your windshield blades when all you came in for was an oil change. They're the investment manager who alerts you to opportunities when you least expect it; the Uber driver who gets you to the airport in a snowstorm and heavy morning traffic on time and without fuss; the father or mother who makes $80K per year but finds a way to put four kids through Ivy League colleges over a ten-year span.

Don't confuse those who assert that they're "responsible people" with those who possess personal responsibleness. Responsible people consider it enough to attend to what others expect of them, while those who possess personal responsibleness attend to what they expect of themselves, first and foremost. Then they go the extra step.

HOW PERSONAL RESPONSIBLENESS APPLIES TO YOU

Care must be taken to not confuse personal responsibleness with selflessness in dealing with others, or when reaching for perfection while accomplishing your own tasks. To better understand this point consider Tracy, identified by her organization as a manager with high potential. As a successful real estate salesperson and single mother of two young daughters, Tracy moves at high speed throughout the workday to make sure all requests made by her boss, customers, and colleagues are completed as expected and on time. At the close of each workday, Tracy typically rushes out of the office, sending herself voicemail reminders while she picks up one daughter from dance and dashes to get the other from basketball practice. Once home, she straightens up the house and maybe squeezes in a load of laundry as she prepares dinner.

Ask Tracy if she scheduled her annual physical or if she regularly exercises, and she'll quickly let you know that she doesn't have time for such things. While Tracy is clearly a good and responsible person and mother, she wouldn't be described as someone who operates with personal responsibleness. This is mainly because she doesn't keep promises to herself in the same way she does with others. Tracy doesn't really view herself as her own agent of control when it comes to people and things that depend on her existence. She runs her life on the basis of her obligations to others; she places obligations to herself, such as her own health, at a lower level of priority. Exercising and eating properly, getting enough sleep, and getting an annual physical exam are all things that those who embody responsibleness do because of their acceptance of control. It's irresponsible of Tracy not to attend to her personal health and stamina. Her kids and job depend on her being healthy. In fact, they would likely be in very bad shape without her. Because of what she doesn't do, Tracy doesn't have personal responsibleness. She may pride herself on being selfless in what she does and in how she goes about doing it, but in the broader scope of what's critically important to both herself and her family, she needs to revise her priorities. No one can do that for her. She must do that for herself.

THE IMPORTANCE OF COMMITMENT AND SELF-DISCIPLINE

Personal responsibleness isn't something that comes naturally to anyone. And no one can reliably tell you or any other person how to get it. It's about committing to a set of standards that become a kind of crossbeam supporting the architecture of all that makes up what a person is and strives to be. This structure includes values, beliefs, attitude, and tenacity in getting things done, how they want to view themselves, and how they want to be seen by others.

Equipping oneself with personal responsibleness is surprisingly simple, though not necessarily easy. It's a matter of making and sticking to commitments to yourself. Think of the wise counsel of one of Shakespeare's characters: "This above all: to thine own self be true" or, on a more practical level, the words of Leonard Cohen, "Act the way you'd like to be and soon you'll be the way you act."

When people accept personal responsibleness, they're not looking at whether a responsibility is theirs. Rather, the focus is on doing whatever is in their control to ensure that something gets done, and a valuable difference results. Not surprisingly, the way that people with personal responsibleness carry out their jobs is not only delightful for those they work with and serve, but also gratifying for themselves because they're setting their own standards and fulfilling obligations to themselves.

ACCEPTING PERSONAL RESPONSIBLENESS

The acceptance of control, which is the main determinant of personal responsibleness, necessarily involves thinking for yourself. Here's a quick line of questioning that provides a valuable insight: When other people give you a task, do you tend to simply complete it as they say? Or do you typically stop and think about how much of what they want is truly within your control and whether or not you can live up to your own, as well as to their expectations? Will you personally need—or be able—to go beyond fulfilling those expectations?

When you operate with personal responsibleness, it becomes important that you're willing to think for yourself, even if that means taking on some occasional opposing views. It also means you're willing to accept the consequences of your decisions and actions without making excuses or blaming others.

The inventory worksheet below focuses on the workplace to give you an insight regarding your acceptance of control for how you think, feel, and act. See it as an opportunity to gain a better understanding of what it means to operate with personal responsibleness.

INVENTORY OF PERSONAL RESPONSIBLENESS AT WORK

(To download this form go to: www.drdebbright.com/
pro-achievement-bonus-page)

Check the response that most accurately reflects what you actually do, not what you think you should do.
1. Never 2. Occasionally 3. Sometimes 4. Frequently
5. Almost Always

		1	2	3	4	5
1.	When your boss tells you to do something with which you totally disagree, do you do it without question?					
2.	As events unfold, you think you're the last to know. Do you feel resentful and complain to others that management isn't keeping you as well informed as it should?					
3.	Someone from another department approaches you in an aggressive and tactless way. Do you let that person's manner determine whether or not you'll cooperate?					
4.	Someone from another department approaches you with a problem. Do you discuss the problem as if the problem were still solely the other person's?					
5.	You're working on a report or project for a peer. Do you submit it even though you think you could do a better job (and still meet the deadline)?					
6.	As a deadline approaches, you're still waiting for information that was promised to you from another department. Do you feel that the failure to deliver the information is a justifiable explanation when your boss questions your progress?					
7.	A peer isn't performing up to standard. Do you avoid saying anything to them for fear of facing a potential confrontation?					

8. When faced with a lack of cooperation from others, do you have difficulty getting tasks done on time.				
9. If no one knew what time you started work, would you sleep later in the morning?				
10. If your boss sets goals that you believe are unrealistic, do you complain to others?				
Scoring and Interpretation Add the numerical value for each response to get your total score. Refer to the following scale for interpretation.				
15 and under - High degree of personal responsibleness				
16 to 21 - Moderate degree of personal responsibleness				
22 to 27 - Low degree of personal responsibleness				
28 and above - Needs improvement				

(To download this form go to: www.drdebbright.com/pro-achievement-bonus-page)

Your score on the "Inventory of Personal Responsibleness at Work" worksheet may depend on the distinction you made between "occasionally," "sometimes," and "frequently." However, the litmus test of personal responsibleness is looking into the mirror and asking, "If I interviewed a prospective employee who thought and felt the way I do about my work and how I approach it, would I hire them?"

Reexamine each of the questions included in the inventory and ask yourself, "What are the parameters of control in this situation?" None of these situations

PRO-ACHIEVEMENT PRINCIPLE

required the introduction of any new policies or proce-
dures. Rather, effectively handling the situations noted
is simply a matter of looking to yourself to take the
control available to you and to live up to the standards
you set for yourself.

Self-examination begins with understanding control and its dimensions. You need to examine what
you want, recognize your abilities and limitations,
and determine how to best utilize your energies. By
recognizing that you are the gateway for formulating what's happening around you and that you hold
the available levers of control, you gain the power of
habitually achieving desired outcomes. You're passing
through the threshold of developing self-reliance as well
as self-confidence, which together are key to reaching
your desired outcomes.

Another aspect of personal responsibleness that's
important to highlight involves the ethical standards
that govern your conduct when completing daily
tasks. Think about your workday. How much time
do you allow yourself to handle personal matters? How
much time do you spend surfing the Internet? Ethics
include taking responsibility for how you use time and
resources. Should you use the company's computer
for your personal needs? Should you photocopy those
flyers for your son's Boy Scout troop on the company's

copier without permission? Should you fudge your expense report? Those choices are within your control.

Employees are often given a lot of independence by their employers, who expect them to act professionally. The company is giving the employee the control handles to operate ethically. A person with personal responsibleness recognizes that their conduct isn't only a matter of making sure that they don't shortchange the company; their reputation and self-respect are at stake. If you cut corners or do something borderline in one area, onlookers think to themselves, *Well, you probably will do the same in other areas, maybe in my area, too.* Even if nothing is said, the intangible ingredients of trust, respect, and credibility are tarnished, and peer relationships become open to questioning. This is not good!

OPERATING WITH PURE WINS AND PURE FAILURES

Setting your own standards and living up to your promises sets you up for understanding the importance of working with pure wins and failures. To better understand what this means, consider an athlete who trains three-to-four hours per day for an upcoming competition. The night before the event he goes to a party, drinks, stays up late, and goes to bed exhausted. At the competition the next day, he loses. When reviewing what happened, can the athlete determine if he had the ability to win? Can the athlete figure out what he needs to do better or differently in order to win in the future? These questions are difficult to answer because the athlete might say or think, "If only I hadn't had so much to drink last night, I could have done better," or "I could have performed better if only I hadn't been so tired." The *ifs* and *buts* blur the athlete's ability to see clearly what contributes to his winning or losing. Instead, when an athlete operates with pure wins and failures, he is saying, "I did everything within my control. If I didn't win, it wasn't because I didn't try or do whatever I could. I didn't win because I wasn't meant to, that's all."

This perspective is very much what Vince Lombardi, legendary Green Bay Packers coach, meant when he said, "Winning isn't everything; it's the only thing." For years, people have misinterpreted Lombardi's famous line to mean that you win at all costs. Players who were coached by Lombardi said he meant that when a football player goes into a game, they go in fully prepared to win and certain they have done all they can to be ready to win. If by chance the team loses, it's only because the other team played better! Failure occurs mainly because of factors that are outside the player's control, ability, or knowledge base.

Failures and setbacks are unfortunate and unintentional. However, they're part of life. What we should mostly concern ourselves with is the repetition of the same failures and setbacks. By understanding control and operating accordingly, we can avoid repeating our mistakes. Although people with personal responsibleness dislike failures and disappointments as much as everyone else, they know they have used control to the best of their ability to make a positive difference. Realistically, what more can people ask of themselves?

PERSONAL RESPONSIBLENESS IN WHAT WE SAY

In the workplace, a lot of emphasis can be put on the importance of accountability. Many of us associate accountability with our work-related tasks. Those who have personal responsibleness extend accountability beyond what they do; they also associate accountability with what they say.

What we say is as important as what we do when it comes to personal responsibleness. When tired and under a lot of pressure, we commonly say inappropriate words. Once out, they can't be taken back. It's only human nature to sometimes be lax with what we say, and the words spoken in those moments of spontaneity are often hurtful to others. Be it at home or in the workplace, if you keep in mind your commitment to personal responsibleness you'll begin, as a matter of habit, to check your impulsive behavior regarding what you do or say *before you act*. As a key aspect of The Pro-Achievement Principle, the self-discipline you impose on yourself in practicing personal responsibleness will save a lot of anguish, hardship, and loss of trust and respect within your relationships over time. All this requires is that you take a moment to consider what's about to be spoken, and to seriously assess the impact those words will have.

As exemplified in this lesson, people with personal responsibleness are not only keeping promises to others, but more importantly, they're also fulfilling obligations to themselves. "Taking control," "performing at high standards," "following through," and "making a difference that adds value" are all phrases that clearly describe someone with personal responsibleness. No leader can survive without it. Because those with personal responsibleness can be counted on, others feel proud to associate with them. Such people are thought of as having backbone and "stick-to-itiveness." Most people would like to be viewed this way and want to know the "secrets" of how they can be. Understanding the true meaning of personal responsibleness moves you well on your way toward learning those secrets and becoming the kind of person people trust and admire.

THERE ARE TWO KINDS OF PEOPLE, THOSE WHO
DO THE WORK AND THOSE WHO TAKE THE
CREDIT. TRY TO BE IN THE FIRST GROUP;
THERE IS LESS COMPETITION THERE.
INDIRA GANDHI

Before going to the next lesson, take a moment to really think about what makes you who you are and what you want to be. At this early stage in your progress toward understanding the rewarding merits of Pro-Achievement, you might want to think of a motto for yourself. Consider that motto a first action thought for attaining the aura of personal responsibleness you want to acquire and for which you'd like to be known.

PICK A MOTTO YOU CAN COMMIT TO

Many organizations use a motto as a representative theme for the values they wish their employees to embrace and for which they want the company to be known. A motto can be used across the enterprise to bring out the best in your employees and to represent your brand to your customers and to the general public.

For instance:

Be all you can be –United States Army

Service Above Self –Rotary International

Just Do It! –Nike

Find your purpose –Grand Canyon University
Do your best –Cub Scouts
Think –IBM
No pain, no gain –Exercise motto
To boldly go where no one has gone before –Star Trek
The road to success is always under construction
    –Anonymous

Now go ahead and put pen to paper for your personal motto, and feel free to change it as you work through the next lessons.

THE GREATEST DAY IN YOUR LIFE AND MINE
IS WHEN WE TAKE TOTAL RESPONSIBILITY
FOR OUR ATTITUDES. THAT'S THE
DAY WE TRULY GROW UP.
JOHN C. MAXWELL

LESSON 2 *Takeaway Points for Review*

- "Personal responsibleness," in contrast to "personal responsibility," signals a virtue in someone's character that's permanent and ingrained rather than situational or temporary.

- People who embody personal responsibleness go about tasks in a way that conveys a sense of ownership; they commonly look to what they can bring to a task that suits their own desired results.

- Personal responsibleness is the driving force behind a person's self-imposed standards of behavior.

- Responsible people consider it enough to attend to what others expect of them, while those who possess personal responsibleness attend to what they expect of themselves as well.

- Never confuse personal responsibleness with selflessness in your dealings with others or with reaching for perfection in dealing with your own tasks.

- Equipping yourself with personal responsibleness is a matter of making and sticking to commitments to yourself.

- Likewise, you're willing to accept the consequences of your decisions without making excuses or blaming others.

- Setting your own standards sets you up for understanding the importance of working with pure wins and failures.

- What we say is as important as what we do.

- Go ahead and put pen to paper for your personal motto.

- Responsibilities are mostly thought of as those kinds of obligations that come and go or are assigned and completed. Responsibleness is the permanent *state of being* a person has in taking on their responsibilities and assignments.

～

The INVENTORY OF PERSONAL RESPONSIBLENESS AT WORK can be downloaded at:

http://www.drdebbright.com/ pro-achievement-bonus-page

Print out and use this quick inventory to check where you and your team members stand as it regards this important pro-achievement attribute. It's a great way for starting the team off on the right track.

LESSON 3
YOUR INTRODUCTION TO THE PRO-ACHIEVEMENT PRINCIPLE

Think about people you know who reliably translate their words into actions and seem to have an uncanny understanding of the control they possess in pursuing tasks and projects. These are the people who have an ever-present ability to consistently make things happen. They're not necessarily the sharpest, most entertaining, or friendliest people you know. Nor are they necessarily the most skilled or gifted. But they're far ahead of most others when it comes to the reliability of their word, trustworthiness, honesty, politeness, and their willingness to go the extra mile when it comes to adding value to their team or their department in whatever way they can. They command respect just by being who they are. And they stand out from most of those with whom they interact and work. They are *Pro-Achievers*.

WHAT IS THE PRO-ACHIEVEMENT PRINCIPLE?

The Pro-Achievement Principle isn't a vague theory or some kind of scientific postulate; it is a specific precept, an ingrained attitude. Simply put, it is the conscious choice to internalize the acceptance of control in whatever one does, and a commitment to adding value to every endeavor.

WHAT YOU GET BY ACHIEVING YOUR GOALS
IS NOT AS IMPORTANT AS WHAT YOU BECOME
BY ACHIEVING YOUR GOALS.
HENRY DAVID THOREAU

WHO IS A PRO-ACHIEVER?

Utilizing the principle stated above, reinforced through discipline and focus, the Pro-Achiever's first consideration is how to add value and go beyond the boundaries of their initial expectations. The Pro-Achiever practices doing things a notch or two better than what their first impulse might suggest; over time, that way of thinking becomes inherent in their every endeavor. Pro-Achievers understand the difference between possessing responsibleness and merely having responsibilities.

Before you can influence others to embrace the principle and the astonishing merits of becoming a Pro-Achiever, it's important to understand what differentiates Pro-Achievers from overachievers and perfectionists.

PRO-ACHIEVERS ARE NOT OVERACHIEVERS

We all know people who somehow seem obsessed with accomplishing certain goals and objectives. Obsessiveness isn't a trait of Pro-Achievers or potential Pro-Achievers. Obsessiveness is a trait of an overachiever. In fact, overachievers will most likely have difficulty becoming Pro-Achievers since they have an entirely different mindset that's nearly the polar opposite of any Pro-Achiever.

For instance, while the overachiever will typically and mindlessly ignore personal needs and responsibilities in relationships to get the job done, the Pro-Achiever never would consider ignoring either of these two elements. Pro-Achievers generally keep themselves in shape, eat the right foods, and stay very close to their friends and family as a matter of priority over everything else. That's because they know people depend on them, and they possess something over-achievers don't have: personal responsibleness.

Overachievers operate mainly with their self-centered objectives and personal expectations in mind. They certainly do have high standards, but their standards are often brutally applied to themselves, team members, coworkers, and direct reports. An obsession with their rigid standards drives them into sometimes irreparable conflicts with others, including family members and trusted friends. Their focus on results obfuscates their awareness of any process in achieving those results. Typically, this type of person may seem pretty good to an employer until that employer sees those traits in action. The main problem with over-achievers is that they're often scared to death of failure and step back from using untried ways to improve their own performance or to help develop the performance of others. When they run into problems for which they have no answer or solution, their fear of failure kicks in, and they typically procrastinate and avoid taking any action at all.

Overachievers are overly eager to please. They thrive on achieving as a way to secure love and approval from the hierarchy. They, rather than the team or any fellow coworkers, are always their own main objective. Overachievers are often the ones who quickly find themselves under their bosses' spotlight for the next promotion to team leader or departmental manager. This type of role is where their faults eventually come to light. They don't share recognition for success because they think of themselves as the main initiator behind most of what goes on under their watch. There's a good reason for this, since they take almost total control of everything down the chain of command for which they're responsible except, of course, failures. For failures, they always manage to find a scapegoat! You don't want overachievers as team leaders or even on your team. They'll wreck the morale and the ambition of other members in no time flat.

PRO-ACHIEVERS ARE NOT PERFECTIONISTS

As you might suspect, overachievers and perfectionists have a lot in common. While overachievers outwardly strive for perfection, there's always a chance they'll eventually learn that perfection in all they do isn't possible. By the time they come to such a realization, however, they may have already dispirited fellow team members, caused irreparable damage to their reputation as a leader, and maybe jeopardized relationships with customers.

Perfectionists, like overachievers, tend to set high goals and work hard toward achieving them. This way of handling things has worked for them most of their lives. They're the ones whose bedrooms were lined with trophies, starting from the time they were kids and continuing right through college. A close look at those trophies will often show that the awards are for non-team-centered activities such as singles tennis, bowling, golf, archery, track and field, and even spelling bees or success with a musical instrument. That's all great, likely well deserved, and highly commendable. People could rightly argue that these kinds of successes mold character and integrity. But too often perfectionists are stubbornly rigid in their ways and persistent when it comes to their own self-imposed standards. Perfectionists accept nothing less than perfection. "Almost perfect" is seen as failure. "A job well done" or "good job" isn't part of the vocabulary of the perfectionist. There certainly is a place for perfectionists in any organization as long as that place isn't on a team or as a team leader.

Bottom line: As with overachievers, don't expect a lot from perfectionists when it comes to team building or sharing glory with others.

IT IS NEVER TOO LATE TO BECOME
WHAT YOU MIGHT HAVE BEEN.
MARY ANN EVANS

THE PRO-ACHIEVER FOCUS

FROM GOOD TO BETTER AND
FROM BETTER TO BEST

As with many things in life, getting what you want out of yourself and your employees is a question of dose and balance. The expectations of how work is undertaken make a tremendous difference when it comes to whether people will or will not enjoy what they do. The Pro-Achievement Principle doesn't involve the expectation of getting "the most" out of yourself or anyone else. What it does involve is promoting added value and making positive differences when doing tasks both large and small.

An aphorism from Confucius's *Analects*—"To go beyond is as wrong as to fall short"—comes close to fitting the idea behind the Principle of Pro-Achievement.

This adding value to things doesn't necessarily mean only important things, big things, or things that people see. It applies to adding value even in small doses and in little ways that make a difference. It applauds actions that result in matters that go from good to better, in a way that's equally significant to those that go from better to best.

The more people practice being conscious of the Principle of Pro-Achievement in what they do, both big and small, the more it becomes a natural impulse of their thinking. And even though there's no applause or award given for their actions that create greater value and make a difference, personal pride and self-respect becomes the payoff they'll come to cherish.

Imagine a team in which each member is committed to making the Principle of Pro-Achievement the foundation of their personal work ethic. Probably the first thing that would become noticeable is the effectiveness of how well members interact with one another. With each having the desire to add value and make a difference in most of what they do, politeness would become more apparent within their interactions. Politeness is an important way of showing respect. Showing respect for others adds value to relationships and can make a huge difference in furthering and maintaining positive relationships. Next, you'd see a heightened degree of cooperation among the group, with each member realizing that the success of the team is dependent upon all members of that group and not just upon the talented few. In time other teams, perhaps in the same organization, would begin noticing the stark contrast between their successes and those of the team operating under The Pro-Achievement Principle—and isn't that the team you want? You can have it. Please read on!

INCORPORATING WORK ETHICS AS CHALLENGES TO CHANGE

The fact that you made the choice to read this particular BIZLET is a pretty good indication that you're seeking ways to improve the performance of yourself, your teammates, and if you're a leader, the people you oversee. If, as a leader, you think the performance level of some of your staff members allows a lot of room for improvement, take solace in the fact that you're not alone. Not everyone has a good work ethic to build on.

According to a recent study examining the productivity of 2,000 office workers conducted by *Inc.* magazine—get ready for this—the average employee is productive only three hours out of an eight-hour day! Where does all that wasted time go? On average, over one hour is spent every day reading news websites, and a whopping forty-four minutes is gobbled up by checking social media. Another forty minutes is spent socializing with other employees about non-work-related topics. Those comprised the top three time-consuming activities. Then there's searching the Internet (twenty-four minutes), unscheduled breaks (twenty-three minutes), and personal calls and text-messaging (thirty-seven minutes). Lunch, drinks, and snacks typically eat up thirty-one minutes of the workday.

Now, maybe you or the people who work with you don't necessarily match the statistics *Inc.* magazine collected in their survey. Nevertheless, use your own observations to decide whether there's room for driving improved individual performance within your teams and reports. Very likely there is.

A WORD ABOUT MILLENIALS AND WORK ETHICS

A lot has been written and said about today's incoming population of first-time employees entering the workforce. Maybe you are one of them or have coworkers who are. Many have noted that some millennials appear to be a breed quite different from previous generations such as the now mostly retired baby boomers. Some older workers have been heard to speak about the millennial generation, namely those born between 1981 and 1996, as having different attitudes toward work or a different "work ethic" that doesn't get the results boomers were able to deliver. There's some evidence to suggest that this is true. In fact, to the extent perceptions count, about two-thirds of employers (63% of business decision makers and 68% of recruiters) say their organizations struggle to manage millennials.

Through her study of millennials entering the workforce, Kathryn Shaw, professor of economics at Stanford Graduate School of Business, found that earning more money as the onset objective of starting a career doesn't have the same broad appeal today as it did in past decades. Today, many new recruits in the workplace are willing to forgo higher pay for a more satisfying work culture. Mark Royal, a senior principal at Korn Ferry, a global organizational consulting firm, noted that young employees who are starting new careers look to link up with a strong brand where they can more readily partake in the company's success and superior training programs. A good majority view this as more important than simply getting a higher starting salary. Royal found that the millennial generation of workers may, in fact, be a lot more thoughtful and deliberate in choosing their careers than any generation before them. The current generation of job seekers must keep up with rapidly changing technologies to prevent their skills from becoming obsolete within a year or two. These job seekers also realize they must be adaptive to changing social mores in order to avoid career potholes as they maneuver the latest politically correct standards held by the organizational powers-that-be.

An increasing number of today's employers are beginning to understand the value of investing in young, new employees, which goes beyond training them in specific technical areas and on-the-job skills.

While understanding that having technical skills is essential, many of today's leaders and managers are expressing a desire for employees to be courageous, to take initiative, and to set their own standards of performance. Interestingly, these managers believe all employees should think for themselves, as opposed to simply being servants of the organization with ambitions limited to pleasing their immediate hierarchy. More and more modern managers are seeking employees who are dependable, who care deeply about adding value to the organization, and whose objectives are not predicated by an "all about me" priority. How to get employees to develop the attributes and achieve the results that today's managers desire remains a major challenge.

Most managers and team leaders know that some job candidates operate with Pro-Achiever characteristics. But few managers have been able to find a recruiting source that clearly identifies such candidates. Nevertheless, managers yearn for employees who take a realistic view of things and who bring solutions to the problems within the workplace.

Managers want employees to view workplace problems as challenges or opportunities rather than as obstacles. They're looking for employees willing to bring up the negative, not to tear down projects, but to seek out the underlying solutions to real issues. What we are talking about is the adoption of a particular kind of attitude that befits the Pro-Achiever.

YOU CAN'T BE THAT KID AT THE TOP OF THE
WATERSLIDE, OVERTHINKING IT. YOU
HAVE TO GO DOWN THE CHUTE.
TINA FEY

LESSON 3 *Takeaway Points for Review*

- Pro-Achievers are way ahead of almost everybody else when it comes to reliability, trust, honesty, politeness, and willingness to go the extra mile.

- Pro-Achievers clearly understand the difference between the meaning of possessing **responsibleness** and having **responsibilities.**

- The Pro-Achievement Principle applies to those who are imbued with an seemingly natural understanding that adding value and going beyond expectations is *the* first consideration.

- Obsessiveness isn't a trait of Pro-Achievers or potential Pro-Achievers.

- As with overachievers, don't expect a lot from perfectionists when it comes to team building or sharing glory with others.

- The Principle of Pro-Achievement involves promoting added value and making positive differences when doing tasks both large and small.

- The more people practice being conscious of the Principle of Pro-Achievement in what they do, both big and small, the more it becomes a habit of their thinking.

- With each person having the desire to add value and make a difference in most of what they do, polite interactions will become more apparent.

- There's value in investing in young new employees that goes beyond training them in technical and on-the-job skills.

- Anyone, at any time, can decide to become a Pro-Achiever. It's a personal choice not limited by title, age, education, or years of experience in the workforce.

~

Reinforce and reenergize the pro-achievement principle for your team each and every month.

The Pro-Achievement Way Monthly Coaching Letter.

This *free, no-obligation* informative monthly letter provides leaders and teams with effective insights for bringing more out of themselves by employing *The Pro-Achievement Principle*™ as their central mantra. This principle is best defined as "the adoption of a personal code of conduct whereby individuals accept control to consistently add an extra degree of value to all that they endeavor."

It's FREE !!
https://www.drdebbright.com/
publications-all/#coaching-letter

LESSON 4
THE IMPORTANCE OF ATTITUDE

You'll be amazed that once you commit to the tenets of personal responsibleness, your attitude will begin to change. Those changes will positively affect personal relationships and how you view yourself as a person who can make things happen. This noticeable transformation of your overall attitude will occur in a way that seems natural and barely deliberate. Remember, personal responsibleness is a state of being whereby, through self-discipline, you begin to develop habitual ways of approaching matters in order to make a valuable difference in your life and the lives of others. This change will find its way into almost everything you do.

Adopting a commitment to personal responsibleness is the key driver that will influence your new perspective, and the main characteristic of that perspective is best defined as an "achieving attitude."

THE GREATEST DISCOVERY OF MY GENERATION IS
THAT A HUMAN BEING CAN ALTER HIS LIFE
BY ALTERING HIS ATTITUDES.
WILLIAM JAMES

WHAT IS MEANT BY AN ACHIEVING ATTITUDE?

Go ask a few people, "What's the difference between a good attitude and a bad attitude?" The answers will surprise you mainly because of their definitional similarity. Most will define the difference within the spectrum of the polarities suggested in your question itself, namely, the extremes of good on one end and bad on the other. Commonly, people associate a "good" attitude as one that's *non-confrontational, supportive, cooperative, positive, can-do, will do,* and, well, anything but negative. "Bad" attitude, on the other hand, would likely be associated with terms that are the opposite of those of a "good" attitude. Of course, none of those answers would be wrong. But when we speak to someone about their attitude, wouldn't it be a lot more helpful if we used words that were more specific in the meaning we're trying to convey? Think about it. If you're told by someone, "You have a bad attitude," or "You know what? You need to improve your attitude," how are you supposed to guess the extent of the changes you need to make in order to meet their expectations?

Very rarely do we hear specific terms for a "good" attitude such as *realistic, thoughtful, caring, mindful, beneficial, helpful,* or *accommodating,* which more accurately describe what we mean when we say someone has a "good attitude." Whether criticizing or praising a person about their attitude, it would be more useful if you said specifically what is good or bad about their attitude.

Besides simply defining it, this lesson introduces the dynamics of the *achieving attitude*, the operative attribute that characterizes the behavior of Pro-Achievers. You'll learn how this important attribute operates in concert with personal responsibleness to complete the full picture of what makes a Pro-Achiever.

THE ACHIEVING ATTITUDE IN ACTION

To get a glimpse at what it means to operate with an achieving attitude as it applies to a Pro-Achiever, meet Gabriel Lopez, a salesperson who works for Jeanie Murrow. Jeanie heads up the sales department for a medical device company with 565 employees headquartered in Nashville, Tennessee. Sitting in her office looking over the monthly sales numbers, Jeanie noticed once again that Gabriel had a quarter that outshone the rest of the sales force. For over a year, Jeanie had been casually observing that Gabriel seemed to do things slightly different from his peers. For instance, Gabriel gets quotes from the finance group faster than anyone else, and he regularly receives full support from the staff, who make it a point to pull his proposals together more quickly than usual. His reports look more polished and professional. Upon reflection, Jeanie has come to realize that Gabriel receives more calls and emails from customers thanking him for the great service they received.

Jeanie's curiosity gets the best of her, so instead of continuing to analyze Gabriel's monthly report, she walks over to Gabriel's cubicle, and says, "Gabe, I want to congratulate you once again for another successful month! Tell me, do you have some secret formula that allows you to excel and close sales so well? Would you mind please sharing with me what you're doing that enables you to receive so much staff support and be so successful?"

A big smile lights up Gabriel's face and without hesitation he replies, "I'd be glad to pass along what I do, and I wish there were a secret formula I could share with you, but there really isn't." He goes on to explain in detail how he operates. After listening to Gabriel for a few minutes, Jeanie drops her jaw in amazement at how much he has learned in the short time he's been in the organization. Jeanie is especially interested to learn that to exceed expectations, Gabriel uses ideas and behaviors of his own creation, which any of her salespeople could adopt. She wonders aloud how and when Gabriel learned these things. Gabriel tells her that he thinks that "servicing" doesn't only mean what he does for the customer. He explains that he can't make a single sale without the help of others within the organization.

This causes Jeanie to flash back to a time when Gabriel needed a quote instantly. Jeanie remembers that when Mary was asked to prepare the quote, she stayed late to get it done. The following morning, Jeanie heard more than once that Gabriel had given Mary a gift card to Starbucks to thank her. She recalled how Gabriel would often go back to his team who helped prepare his proposals to let them know the outcome of the sale. And the team would cheer! Gabriel not only pointed out what made the proposal stand out, but on occasion, offered a few suggestions for what could be done even better. While Jeanie is certain the other reps thank the staff as Gabriel does, few of them take the time to let the team know how their contribution made a valuable difference that resulted in a successful sale.

Jeanie also learns that Gabriel makes it a point to always remember to use the person's name when speaking to them, and he shows a genuine interest in what they're saying during every conversation. Frequently, Gabriel stops to say hello to the support staff, instead of bypassing them as he walks to the break room. Finally, Gabriel's interest in customers is obvious to them. Quite often, Gabriel initiates a call within a week of making a sale to check on how the customer is doing.

Jeanie thanked Gabriel for his willingness to share his thoughts, and, while walking back to her office, she kept thinking about Gabriel's attitude and how he appeared so committed to dig in and face reality. She remembered him telling her once that when his sales activity starts slipping, he takes it on as a personal challenge and follows up with prospects to encourage a yes or no decision.

On her drive home that day, Jeanie imagined what it would be like if all her sales team adopted Gabriel's productive attitude. She wondered how to encourage other sales reps to be more like Gabriel. Would it simply involve introducing the other reps to how Gabriel views his job and gains the support of the service staff? Is Jeanie's thinking on the right track? Or is she being unrealistic and too simplistic about getting most of her sales staff to operate with Gabriel's work ethic and energy?

Jeanie is on the right track. But the hard work to get each of her staff to operate as Gabriel does isn't entirely up to her. And while Gabriel can help by sharing his methods with other salespeople, he can do little more. The heavy lifting is up to each individual on her team. All that's required of each of them is to put their attitudinal habits aside for a while and commit to opening themselves to learning how they can make a valuable difference. They could do this by first adopting a willingness to accept the change that's within their control (personal responsibleness) and then committing, as Gabriel had, to making a valuable difference (achieving attitude).

I DO NOT TRY TO DANCE BETTER THAN ANYONE ELSE.
I ONLY TRY TO DANCE BETTER THAN MYSELF.
MIKHAIL BARYSHNIKOV

BECOMING A PRO-ACHIEVER

What Gabriel best exemplifies in the previous scene is an *achieving attitude,* the vital ingredient that, when coupled with personal responsibleness, makes up the very nature of a Pro-Achiever.

Similar to how personal responsibleness involves our acceptance of what we can and cannot control, so too must we accept the control regarding our attitudes at any given time.

The moment that *achieving attitude* combines with *personal responsibleness,* a process begins that results in consistently adding value. Pro-Achievers operate with this understanding until it becomes habitual. As with most habits, in time it becomes something of which they're only partially aware.

ATTITUDES ARE NOT BELIEFS

Attitudes tend to be at the surface of our conscious awareness and not as deeply rooted as are firm beliefs. Beliefs are more steadfast than attitudes. For instance, you might hear someone say, "I've always voted Republican (belief) but I like that Democratic senator from Massachusetts (attitude)." There can be certain beliefs we have about people, brands, styles, and personalities that, while we may not be sure where such beliefs come from, we consider them to be reliable. For instance, we may extend a level of trust to a person because we *believe* that anybody who looks us in the eye is trustworthy. Hmm, valid? Probably not. Many, if not most of us, don't check out the validity of our beliefs because we rely on our "gut feelings" or something a parent or close friend told us in the past. But a good portion of our beliefs are rooted in our experiences. Over time, these experiences may become only vague recollections while the beliefs they established remain strong.

On the other hand, we find our attitudes easily defensible. We understand why we adopt them, where they come from, and we are generally flexible about altering them. They seem to take shape more immediately than our beliefs. We know and perhaps more easily accept what we feel.

An important tenet to keep in mind is that you're in control of your attitudes, and you're the one who ultimately changes them. Pay attention to your attitudes and what they're doing for and to you. Remember that only you truly know your own attitudes. Everyone else surmises them, from your actions, words, et al. And regardless of how little or well others know you, surmise them they will.

People have the ability to signal their attitudes in a variety of ways. Of course, verbalizing likes and dislikes is a pretty good indication of the attitude someone has. So are nonverbal cues such as facial expressions, eye rolling, posture, leaning on the car horn for more than two seconds, or silence where some sort of feedback may be expected. Silence, in fact, may be surmised and interpreted as intended feedback, left to the receiver to guess whether it is negative or not!

Within the experiences of our personal and business relationships, we become familiar with how the people around us signal their attitudes about different things. It might be something barely observable such as a wrinkling of the nose when you ask, "How about fish tonight?" On the other hand, some people may possess such a wide range of attitudes that we never gain a comprehensive understanding of them all.

In any case, over time, each of us accumulates and processes impressions that we use to signal those we work or live with. Those signals tend to put us in an attitudinal category that contributes to our reputation. See if you recognize people you work with who fit one of the following dominant attitudinal styles.

THE NEGATIVIST

These people often seem to relish reading or hearing bad news. At work, they huddle with their buddies around the water fountain, whining about management's latest decision or questioning aloud why management is opting for a particular course of action. That's their right in our free country, but what are they accomplishing? If an action fails, they're the first to say, "I told you so." These people tend to converse exclusively with others who are like-minded and who feel equally powerless when it comes to creating solutions. Given a chance to express their opinions to someone who has the power to change things, they typically get weak-kneed. Any ideas they put forth are often poorly thought out or impractical. To explain their reluctance to try to improve things, these people commonly say things like, "It's no use," "No one will listen," "It won't make any difference in the long run," or "For what? So my boss gets the credit?"

Whether at work or in a social setting, the Negativist saps the energy of everyone in the group by frequently criticizing and raising doubts. Questioning and introducing valid criticisms can be helpful, especially when coupled with a willingness to consider what can be done to remedy the situation. But the Negativist's persistent criticisms are not designed to either reveal or solve problems or to produce change; intentionally or not, they tend to disrupt things and tear at the fabric of morale.

THE ENTITLIST

Closely associated with Negativists are the Entitlists. These people always look out for "numero uno." Projects or tasks are engaged in mainly for personal benefit. In the workplace, Entitlists are quick to ask for a promotion or raise. Their state of mind can best be described as "deserving." Yet, when asked what they've done to deserve the raise or promotion, they usually cannot come up with concrete examples. Still, that doesn't discourage them from persisting. Entitlists see themselves as being "owed" things. They usually discount anyone's effort to help them, and rarely do they thank others. Their failure to show appreciation is typically not a matter of poor manners. It's simply a reflection of their attitude, which focuses entirely on themselves and what they want, need, or feel they deserve.

THE SUPERFICIAL OPTIMIST

At the opposite end of the attitudinal spectrum from Negativists are those commonly identified as "easy to get along with." These people are typically cheerful and enthusiastic. They certainly have a place in any organization. But that place should never be a leadership position. Their first and unspoken objective is to be liked at all costs. Their cause often appears to be that they want everyone to be upbeat; they go out of their way to take center stage in coalescing the group, as if it were their personal responsibility. Their cause is always considered a worthy one but, unfortunately, their efforts and ideas rarely make a difference when it comes to changing anything. They're often the first to be nominated "Departmental Person of the Year" because they have such a "positive attitude."

Thinking positively is a good characteristic. But a Superficial Optimist goes beyond the positive thinker in their belief that fate plays a part in the outcome of events. They feel comfortable in accepting mostly all changing conditions as the "new normal" requiring adaptation rather than scrutiny. Hoping for beneficial change is even more important to them than creating beneficial change. Similarly, they don't critically examine their own circumstances. They're not realists. They see what they want to see. They have difficulty handling the truth. The Superficial Optimist is the baseball fan still cheering for the home team when the score is nine to two with two outs and no one on base at the bottom of the ninth.

In the workplace, the Superficial Optimist rarely, if ever, points to anything the department, team, or company could do better. Eventually, they gain a reputation among peers as having low credibility and an absence of fortitude. Often called the "company cheerleader," the Superficial Optimist is, unfortunately, frequently viewed by upper management as an obvious candidate for promotion mainly because nothing objectionable appears in their performance appraisals. Superficial Optimists are often considered safe bets for awards and promotions because they never rock the boat and have loads of fans. They should never be considered for leadership positions.

THE PRO-ACHIEVER

Because of their persistent efforts to habituate a commitment to making a valuable difference in all they set out to do, Pro-Achievers can demonstrate attitudes that reflect hints of other styles. But no particular style dominates enough to result in a categorical identity that translates into a reputation. Pro-Achievers' attitudes spring from their rooted commitment to personal responsibleness. They can show the enthusiasm and energy of the Superficial Optimist, but they also look at things critically, much like the Negativist would, to uncover problems and discover root causes. In a word, *improvement* is their constant motive. They consistently make things happen; they're persistent, determined, and disciplined. Pro-Achievers are the people you feel you can always count on. They don't do things for personal gain like Entitlists. Rather, they're genuinely interested in making a valuable difference for the team, project, and the organization. They look out for themselves but never make it *about* themselves.

There are some aspects of the Pro-Achiever that you cannot see. Besides being able to get things done, they always keep in mind the interests of everyone else, not merely their own. They operate with the three essential characteristics that differentiate them from others:

- They are rooted in realism.

- They view problems not as obstacles, but as challenges and opportunities.

- They consistently strive to make a valuable difference.

NEVER MISTAKE MOODS FOR ATTITUDES

Remember, only you know your attitudes; everyone else surmises them. This is why mood and attitude should not be confused. A mood is an emotional state. It's situational and considerably closer to the surface of your consciousness than your attitude. Your mood is the thing that's most easily seen or heard by those around you. Mood can easily be interpreted from small outward signs, whereas you have to intentionally communicate for someone to know your true attitude.

Consider the following scenario to help differentiate mood and attitude: You're eating your favorite ice cream cone while driving your car. The ice cream melts faster than you can eat it, so it drips all over your clothes and your car seat. What's your mood? (Likely bad.) Will your attitude toward ice cream change? (Likely not.) As this shows, your mood encompasses your feelings at a given moment, whereas your attitude is more enduring.

As Dr. David Burns points out in his book, *Feeling Good*, your mood results from your thinking. But changing your mood by thinking is usually not so easy; it takes work and commitment. Changing your mood is a good exercise as you start toward your objective of becoming a Pro-Achiever. In fact, you can keep your Pro-Achiever mental muscles in shape by being aware of your moods and trying to change them, if necessary. We all know that it's not easy to put on a fake smile and wait to see a cheery self emerge. You need to understand how to take control and work with yourself to use your thinking and your mannerisms to counteract an emotional state such as your mood. The more you succeed in changing your mood, the more you'll come to realize the control you have over your thoughts and attitudes.

HOW TO CONTROL YOUR MOODS

It's logical to conclude that an attitude can override a bad mood, since mood is an emotion and even more at the surface of our thinking than an attitude. When Olivia, the owner of a women's consignment dress shop, wakes up in a bad mood she's able to "shake it off." Olivia has the attitude that she can and should exert a positive influence on the staff and customers she interacts with daily at her store. Before she leaves her house she tells herself, "I can't arrive at work in a toxic mood, and if I don't change it, no one else is going to, so get a grip." And off to work she goes with a spirit that will help her rather than hinder her in making a valuable difference in what she does at work that day.

Changing your mood involves being willing to adjust how you're thinking and feeling at a given moment and then reinforcing what you're thinking with actions. As Dr. Harry Croft, a Distinguished Life Fellow of the American Psychiatric Association, explains to his patients, "An airline pilot has to have an attitude of *safety first* and total concentration on what they're doing, regardless of whether they had a serious argument with their spouse before leaving home that day. Like the pilot, you need to be able to draw upon something bigger than your mood . . . And that's your attitude."

HOW TO CONTROL YOUR ATTITUDE

Consider an everyday example that illustrates how easily you can control your attitude: Imagine yourself talking to a co-worker on the phone at work. Your attitude toward the person is negative, and the subject being discussed is controversial, so much so that you lose patience. You're in the middle of telling off the person on the phone when the other telephone rings.

It's an important client. You drop the call with the colleague you don't like, pick up the new call, and quite effortlessly say hello in a pleasant and welcoming tone. What happened to your negative attitude? You hung up on that attitude as easily as you dropped the call with your colleague.

Sometimes we mask our attitude and behave contrary to how we feel. Who doesn't have an annoying relative, with whom we feel obligated to be pleasant? We smile when we need to smile, and we strike up casual conversation to maintain harmony. The situation is more challenging when we don't like a boss with whom we need to interact regularly. We have to keep our jobs because we need the money. We invest a lot of energy to get along with that boss. And we do so even though deep down inside, we still view that boss negatively.

Masking your attitude is possible, although it's difficult to do for long. Knowing it can be done, however, establishes a good, clear example of the control we can have over our attitude.

DEALING WITH THE ATTITUDES AND EMOTIONS OF OTHERS

When it comes to how we characterize the attitudes of others, we tend to quickly describe them as having a negative attitude, a wait-and-see attitude, a lazy attitude, a winning attitude, a selfish attitude, a positive attitude, and so on. In applying such labels, we usually take into consideration what we know about a person's past, something that person has said, or what we've observed about that person's behavior and mannerisms. We use that information to neatly categorize them. As our own attitude toward that person develops further, we may come to realize that our labeling of the person's presumed attitude may be wrong.

Here's a familiar situation regarding the inability to assess other people's attitudes accurately. It's apparent to everyone in the office that Sherry is having difficulties performing her job, even though she seems to have the required skills. After being transferred to another department, Sherry blossoms. Around the coffee machine, coworkers speculate about what made the difference: Was the problem the dynamics between Sherry and her former boss? Is the new boss responsible for the improvements? Or did the employee, Sherry, change her attitude herself sans the influence of anyone else? In those situations, we, as onlookers, can never know for sure. That is, until Sherry reveals the truth for us.

CONSIDER ATTITUDE WHEN HIRING

The impossibility of knowing for sure is the very reason some human resources professionals are reluctant to use attitude as a primary criterion for measuring performance or for hiring new employees. One human resources executive put it this way, "When hiring, the HR professional's primary concern has been, and still is, that the candidate meets the appropriate job requirements, such as degrees, credentials, experience, and necessary skill sets. The hiring manager, on the other hand, wants the candidate to have the needed skills but also desires to know what it will be like to work with the potential hire. This distinction brings to the forefront that the role of an HR professional is quite different from that of a hiring manager. In a broad sense, HR professionals have a keen awareness of their responsibility to keep the company out of court. Dealing with attitude as a measure of qualification is much too subjective for inclusion in their recommendation for hiring. HR professionals are understandably uncomfortable working with attitude because their mandate is to work with empirical data.

Understanding how important attitude is in developing better relationships with others and better outcomes at home and at work requires exploring the role that attitude plays in forming make-or-break perceptions about ourselves and others. For example, you're interviewing two candidates for an entry-level sales position in your organization. Both candidates have graduated from college with honors. Both have had minimal work experience. Yet during the interview, Candidate 2 talks enthusiastically about the position and she expresses her desire to do whatever is necessary to make the department succeed. During the interview, she asks pertinent questions regarding what her responsibilities will be. At the end of the interview, she politely thanks you as she exits. Candidate 1 professes to really want this position but seems aloof. Talking with Candidate 1 is rather difficult because you have to pull information from him as he answers questions deliberately and with little enthusiasm. When asking questions of Candidate 2, you feel at ease as she helps to carry the conversation, and she expresses enthusiasm while providing relevant examples that relate back to her experience while completing her degree. Candidate 1 asks questions that relate more to how many hours he is expected to work and when he is eligible for vacation. While these are relevant questions, they do cause you to consider what his priorities are. In the end, chances are great that your perceived notion of Candidate 2's attitude will play a part in making your hiring decision.

Increasingly, HR professionals are coming to recognize that attitudes in the workplace are important not only in the hiring process but also as a consideration for promotion. "Whether we want to admit it or not," as one HR director noted, attitudes can be the determining factor in deciding who gets promoted. The attitude factor is typically part of the informal company system. While we're reluctant to put attitude in the performance appraisal process because it's so hard to measure, that doesn't mean we believe attitude isn't important. Quite the contrary. Most would prefer working with someone who has a good attitude, but is weak in certain skill areas, rather than the reverse. It's easier to strengthen someone's skills than to change a bad attitude."

Many managers share that opinion. Developing good working relationships with peers and employees is of high importance. Studies have shown that few managers feel qualified to coach employees on attitudes and their effect on performance. Nevertheless, so many of the judgments both HR professionals and managers make about hiring and promoting are quietly based on the perception of attitude.

It's only natural to observe the action, tone of voice, facial expressions, and body language of the people we encounter, as well as evaluate what they say and do. Categorizing people as having a certain attitude enables us to anticipate their actions and reactions so we can be better prepared and feel more in control as new situations arise. While we use our conclusions about peoples' attitudes in predicting their future actions and reactions, we can only surmise what a person's attitude is; only the individual knows for sure.

People's attitudes are constantly being revealed to us. Driving to work in the morning you read bumper stickers that speak of drivers' attitudes regarding politics, sports, guns, police: "Thank a Cop," "Bernie!", and even society in general, "Up Yours!" On the streets and maybe even in the office, baseball caps showing favorite teams, tattoos, T-shirts, torn jeans, caps worn backwards, pink hair, nose rings, and posters are all personal signals people use to telegraph their attitude about something or anything. From these telltale signs we draw conclusions, correctly or incorrectly, and from those conclusions our attitudes about people form, like it or not.

In conclusion, the importance of understanding the role of attitude and its place in the genome of Pro-Achievement goes far beyond job interviews and career success. It's what drives our judgements of others and allows us to be open to ideas that can be useful in changing things for the better. By controlling our attitudes, we become better able to maximize our effectiveness in working with others and gaining their respect and trust.

COCK YOUR HATS—ANGLES ARE ATTITUDES.
FRANK SINATRA

BE MINDFUL OF PRO-ACHIEVER HABITS THAT MAKE A DIFFERENCE

Pro-Achievers understand that to achieve what they want, need, or desire, they must accept control of their actions and take control of the way they think and feel about both themselves and what they're pursuing.

As Gabriel demonstrated earlier in this lesson, Pro-Achievers know that to be consistently successful, they need help and support from others. Saying thank you and offering a token of gratitude is nice and could be interpreted as simply going through the motions or following a standard protocol. What separates Gabriel so well is that he'll take the extra step to consistently make a valuable difference. As in the situation where Mary helped him out at the last minute, Gabriel didn't just thank Mary. He knew that she really liked Starbucks, so he made the effort to thank her in a meaningful way that would resonate with her.

Addressing people by name is a small thing that makes people feel recognized in an important way. The same is true of clearly giving people credit for their work and effort. Stopping by to engage someone in casual chats shows a caring attitude and demonstrates your intention of being friendly even when you have nothing to immediately gain. Letting a staff person know exactly how their effort positively contributed to a project leaves them with a sense of satisfaction of knowing that what they did had made a distinct and valuable difference. Also, pointing out how their work was less than satisfactory is important because it creates a learning opportunity for what could be done better the next time around.

When customers call, be like Gabriel. Help them with their immediate request and take that extra step of remembering their last purchase and making sure that it's continuing to serve them well. Ask what you can do to help them. Gabriel knows that it's not enough to sell the product; he wants to make the customer feel important.

Being rooted in a kind of realism that seeks out problems and views them as challenges, not obstacles, is what separates Pro-Achievers from Superficial Optimists. For example, a Superficial Optimist, upon hearing that the company had a successful year, gets excited and boasts about it to family and friends. A Pro-Achiever, on the other hand, gets as excited as the Superficial Optimist, but realizes that a company's success is no more secure from one year to the next than is a sports team's from season to season. A

Pro-Achiever builds on the company's successful year and proactively sets to work on goals and objectives for the upcoming year.

If, on the other hand, Gabriel sees his sales numbers are down, rather than make excuses to himself or others, he looks to himself and has one of those internal conversations that results in getting himself fired up and back on track.

Become one of the Pro-Achievers who looks out for others as well as themselves. That perspective is an integral part of multidimensional thinking we've seen in some of our nation's top leaders and CEOs. When we forgo our own desires for what others want, we aren't necessarily "giving in" to others or "giving up" something. Rather, we're electing to invest in relationships that may ultimately yield a more enduring sense of fulfillment.

Abiding by the standards of Pro-Achievers will, before you know it, form the foundation of good habits that create amazing opportunities for you and strengthen your relations with coworkers, family members, friends, and even passing strangers. Try always to be mindful of taking that extra step that could make the difference between what's expected and what's appreciated. They can be meaningful little steps practiced in the home, at the office, at the gym, or anywhere else life brings you.

Here is a kind of at-home example that may initially sound simple, but can mean a lot to two people on this big earth:

Lumi wants to go to the movies. Her boyfriend, Jared, was looking forward to attending a sporting event at that same time. Jared is a Pro-Achiever. He agrees to go to the movies and doesn't harbor any resentment because, as a Pro-Achiever, he accepts control for his decisions and operates with no regrets. Although it may seem to others that he is simply relenting, Jared is actually investing in this relationship that's very important to him. He knows that, had he expressed to Lumi that the sporting event was very important to him, she would have certainly agreed to join him there instead of insisting on the movies.

You see, Pro-Achieving can also lead to yielding to others' desires because it may enrich an important relationship. It's not about keeping score, but more about owning the decision to accept or relinquish control.

LESSON 4 *Takeaway Points for Review*

- Once you commit to the tenets of personal responsibleness, you can expect your attitude to change in ways that will positively affect your relationships and your view of yourself as a person who can make things happen.

- An *achieving attitude* is the vital ingredient that, when coupled with personal responsibleness, makes up the very nature of a Pro-Achiever.

- Attitudes tend to be more at the surface of our awareness and not as deeply rooted as our beliefs.

- Negativists' persistent criticisms aren't designed to reveal problems or to produce change; rather, intentionally or not, they tend to disrupt things and detract from a company's culture.

- Entitlists see themselves as being "owed" things. They usually discount anyone's effort to help them, and rarely do they thank others.

- Superficial Optimists certainly have a place in any organization. But that should never be in a leadership position. Their first and unspoken objective is to be liked at all costs. Their cause is always considered a worthy one but, unfortunately, their efforts and ideas rarely make a difference when it comes to changing anything.

- Being rooted in a kind of realism that seeks out problems and views them as opportunities separates Pro-Achievers from Superficial Optimists.

- Pro-Achievers' attitudes spring from their rooted commitment to personal responsibleness. While showing the enthusiasm and energy of the Superficial Optimist, they also look at things critically like the Negativist would, but to uncover problems and discover root causes.

- Pro-Achievers are the people you feel you can always count on. They consistently make things happen; they're persistent, determined, and disciplined. They don't do things for personal gain like Entitlists. They're genuinely interested in making a valuable difference for the team, the project, and the organization.

- Remember, only you know your attitudes. Your mood is the thing that's easily seen or heard by those around you, whereas you must explicitly reveal your attitude.

- By practicing the control we have over our attitudes, we become able to maximize our effectiveness in working with others and gaining their respect and trust.

- The role of an HR professional is quite different from that of a hiring manager. Dealing with attitude as a measure of qualification is too subjective for HR professionals; hiring managers value attitude to better understand what someone will be like to work with.

- Pro-Achievers understand that they must accept control of their actions and take control of the way they think and feel about themselves and what they're trying to pursue.

- Letting staff know how their effort and work has impacted a project, whether by contributing to or detracting from it, gives the person a sense of satisfaction or creates a learning opportunity .

- Abiding by the standards of Pro-Achievers will help you develop beneficial habits that strengthen your relations with coworkers, family, friends, and even strangers.

- Try always to be mindful of taking that extra step. It will fill the gap between what's expected and what's appreciated as something extra.

~

LESSON 5

RECRUITING PRO-ACHIEVERS:
A TEAM LEADER'S GUIDE

Having an open position within your department, team, or whatever venture you might be overseeing should be considered a golden opportunity to hire a Pro-Achiever. Any vacant position can add stress to members of the team; dragging your feet in filling a critical position not only adds to that stress but may threaten customer retention in the process. Fumbling the opportunity by hiring the wrong candidate is highly likely to compound problems. Settling for a mediocre hire should not be necessary once you learn the salient traits and work ethics of a Pro-Achieving employee. By understanding the characteristics of a Pro-Achiever, you'll know better what to look for in every candidate.

However, be prepared to be disappointed. Many interviewees don't measure up as possible Pro-Achievers. Expect those in HR who are screening resumes to *not* have as clear an idea as you do of what Pro-Achiever traits are. Your priorities may be quite different from HR's, whose focus is more on skills and experience. Your mission is to find an individual who has not only the proper skills and knowledge to become a contributing member of the team but also the insight to make a valuable difference every step of the way. Most certainly, HR professionals can help you screen qualified candidates, but you need to take the process a couple of steps further.

In addition to vetting each candidate for general competency, you'll want to focus on individual character, attitude, and willingness to accept control. Uncovering these qualities requires a modest investment of time to set up an effective interview process. By carefully formulating meaningful interview questions (free of any potential matters of litigation) and listening closely to the answers, you'll gain insight into which candidates have the potential to be Pro-Achievers. This is critical. After all, who you hire can either make life easier for you and others on your team or become your worst nightmare, causing you undue stress and frustration. The good news is that all of this is within your control! To get started, consider establishing a sequence of steps designed to fulfill specific objectives. Following are definitive steps that have proven effective.

HIRING PEOPLE IS AN ART, NOT A SCIENCE, AND RESUMES CAN'T TELL YOU WHETHER SOMEONE WILL FIT INTO YOUR COMPANY'S CULTURE.
HOWARD SCHULTZ

Step 1: Review resumes carefully prior to interviews, making notes along the way. Try to get an idea whether the resume reflects a candidate who completed goals. This simple step involves checking and verifying if the person completed high school, college (two-year or four-year program), or a particular certification. If there appear to be gaps in time within the start-to-end continuum, highlight that gap for questioning. But never jump to conclusions with matters like gaps. For example, take Ron, a candidate applying at a packing plant. He apparently quit junior college after one year and resumed his studies two years later. Although at first glance this might seem cause for concern, the interview revealed that he took time out to care for his ailing mother and successfully fulfilled his obligations regarding her care, including the sad task of arranging funeral services. That done, he returned to school and completed his degree. The objective here was to determine if the candidate exhibited enough self-control and determination to see things through to completion in his personal life. Ron's situation gave credence to the possibility that he instinctively operates with Pro-Achiever traits.

The step of reviewing the resume could easily be delegated to someone else. Even Step 2, the phone interview, could be handled by someone other than yourself.

Step 2: Set up a phone interview. If the position requires interaction with others, such as with customers or colleagues, it's important to screen candidates for their phone presence and the ability to use proper grammar and speak clearly. To achieve this objective, a phone interview may be all that's necessary. A brief phone conversation is efficient, convenient, and costs nothing. To leverage the phone interview, interviewers could refer to the applicant's resume (as was described in Step 1) to inquire whether the candidate completed the endeavors pursued. If the candidate states that they completed a college or trade school program, that's duly noted. If the candidate dropped out of school for a reasonable and acceptable reason, such as to help an aging parent or to serve in the military, it's important to note to what extent the candidate successfully fulfilled that obligation. By the way, consider giving "extra credit" to candidates who paid their own way through school, served in the military, or worked for a social cause they truly believed in. Another admirable trait might be that they worked to help with family income.

A phone conversation can provide a solid impression about a candidate's initiative and sense of self-discipline toward completing endeavors and fulfilling responsibilities. During a phone interview, explore what the candidate is most proud of achieving and the difficulties experienced during the process. That conversation may offer insight into what the candidate considers "working hard" and whether the candidate tends to be more about self as opposed to being interested in the broader value derived from the effort. Pay particular attention to whether or not the candidate easily gives credit to others regarding some of their more noted accomplishments.

Though not scientifically based, consider developing a system of point values to associate with each candidate's answers to questions. This can help distinguish one candidate from another. A point system assists in recalling why you assigned extra points and what stood out about each candidate.

Step 3: Set an assignment. Ask the candidate to complete a short, non-work-related assignment by a specific date and time. For example, you might ask candidates to write a brief explanation of why they're interested in the position, given what they know of the job thus far. You can introduce this during the phone interview. Be sure to set a deadline for the assignment, then offer no additional information. Consider having the candidate e-mail the assignment to you or a colleague. It's important to leave it up to the candidate to figure out how to get the assignment completed and sent to the appropriate contact person. This simple task tests to see if the candidate thinks clearly under pressure and can anticipate what's needed to complete assignments. Very importantly, it determines whether the candidate takes initiative to ask the right people to gather the necessary information. And—oh yes, give them your congrats if the assignment is well written. Pay particular attention to the command of grammar and punctuation. While it may not be perfect, keep in mind that Pro-Achievers are not perfectionists. More importantly, if any of the candidates miss the deadline for whatever reason, then it's best to disqualify them. If the assignment was handled correctly and delivered on time, then consider the quality of the write-up. If the position requires a high proficiency of writing skills, the hiring manager should examine the candidate's writing ability closely.

At this stage, watch out for settling for second best. As one highly successful HR executive explained, "What you see is what you get. When hiring, you want the best candidate possible, not someone you believe can be 'developed' for the job. That should never be the focus during the initial screening process of candidates." However, if a manager is in a real pinch and has to hire right away, it's valuable to remember, as this HR executive posited, "It's much harder to train a candidate to have a good attitude, to work well with others, and to not put self-interests above what's best for the company than it is to train that person in technical skills."

Keep in mind that whoever conducts the initial phone interview and sets the assignment can be someone other than yourself; ideally, the phone interviewer should be someone familiar with The Pro-Achiever Principle, who has the lessons of this BIZLET in mind. For consistency's sake, it's best to use the same person for Steps 2 and 3 of each position for which interviews are being conducted. Have the person who handles those steps complete a short form (see sample questions 1-3 below) that captures what they learned from the candidate.

Step 4: In-person interview. Once a candidate completes the assignment on time and submits an acceptable write-up, move to Step 4, the in-person interview. Does the candidate arrive on time? If the candidate is running late, pay close attention to what that candidate does. Make sure the candidate's actions meet your expectations. Look for signs of a Pro-Achiever. Does the person call, text, or e-mail to let you know about a late arrival? Is the late arrival handled in a way that seems reasonable and considerate?

Consider intentionally arriving ten minutes late for the interview and causing the candidate to wait. This strategy may not appeal to some interviewers, but they shouldn't disregard it too quickly. Should you wish to give this strategy a try, you'll find it to be a good early indication of how the candidate uses time. If the candidate will be waiting in the lobby, instruct the receptionist to take note of what the candidate does while waiting for you to arrive. Did they stare at the ceiling in the waiting area? Or, did they use the time in a somewhat productive way such as dealing with messages on their cell phone or reading something about the company? One CEO recalls how one administrative assistant candidate, applying to a small Midwest construction company, called him twice during the ten-minute lapse to learn his whereabouts.

The candidate's phone calls were enough to turn him off. You'll learn a lot about the candidate's social aplomb in handling the unexpected—in this case, your lateness. Are they looking rather upset because you've inconvenienced them, or do they appear to roll with the situation, giving you the benefit of the doubt?

For those positions where an in-person interview is preferred over a written test, it's important that the interview questions address specific job requirements. Has the interviewee taken the initiative to fully understand the job he or she is applying for? Have they crafted useful or insightful questions about the position? Carefully constructed interview questions, such as those that follow, will provide you and the hiring team with valuable insights about the candidate.

HIRE AN ATTITUDE, NOT JUST
EXPERIENCE AND QUALIFICATION.
GREG SAVAGE

INTERVIEW QUESTIONS

Here are a few questions that managers have found revealing about whether the candidate accepts control and operates with an achieving attitude. Asking these questions creates an opportunity for characteristics of a Pro-Achiever to surface.

Interview Question 1: If you were to select an ideal coworker, what characteristics would you look for in this person?

If the candidate has previous job experience, you can revise the question by asking, "Of the coworkers you worked with, what characteristics did you most admire?" Try to get the candidate to produce at least three characteristics or qualities and to explain why as well as what.

Interview Question 2: What would you do in the following situation? You're a server at a restaurant. It's lunchtime, and the restaurant is crowded. You come out of the kitchen and notice that the hostess seated two customers who arrived apparently at the same time and seated them each alone at their respective tables. On the left, the hostess seated a gentleman you recognize as a regular and someone you know to be a poor tipper. On the right, she seated a well-dressed man you don't recognize but who appears "polished." Whom do you wait on first, and how do you handle the situation?

Purpose and Value: Keep in mind, there is really no correct answer. What you're looking for primarily is whether the candidate places their own self-interest above everything else. If the candidate says, "I would wait on the 'polished' person first because maybe I'll get a bigger tip," and elaborates no further, that's a concern. If the candidate says, "We need the regular, but I know he'll keep coming, so I'll wait on the new person first," make sure you ask for an elaboration. Listen very carefully to the explanation. Watch for self-focus over interest in helping the customer and the restaurant. Pay attention to whether the candidate mentions concern for the customer and how important it is to provide a positive experience, so they'll return. Is there any mention of the restaurant itself and its well-being?

Don't be so concerned about probing the candidate to learn more about their thinking. Sometimes, candidates will respond creatively and explain, "Well, if he's a regular I probably know what he likes to eat, so I could acknowledge the regular and ask, 'the usual?' as I'm walking over to greet the new customer. So, I guess I'd address them at the same time." That response is fine. No concerns there. After they fully explain the reasons behind their choice, reflect on whether their focus remained fixed on the customers' satisfaction, which is indicative of the *micro perspective*. Consider if their response included any reference to the growth or stability of the restaurant and its reputation, which is indicative of the *macro perspective* or the bigger picture. Both are valuable perspectives.

What you should make note of is whether the candidate operates with a sense of satisfying the needs of others and the organization. Are both perspectives present? Does the candidate take actions consistent with addressing customer needs while keeping the company's or restaurant's best interests in mind? You can gain some valuable clues about whether the candidate makes a practice of seeing the *micro* while, at the same time, holding onto the *macro* or big picture. Most importantly, does the candidate put self-interest above everything else? If so, that's not a good sign.

Interview Question 3: What would you do in the following situation? You finally get an appointment with your doctor after waiting several weeks. It takes you forty-five minutes to get through traffic, but you arrive on time. After waiting for only a couple of minutes, the nurse comes out and tells you that the doctor is going to be detained for about an hour. What do you do?

Purpose and Value: Again, there's no right answer. You're seeking to learn how the candidate thinks. In this case, you'll begin to discover the candidate's priorities and how they use their time. The candidate might say, "It depends on what's going on at work. If it's a busy day, I might have to set up another appointment." Another response might be, "If it took me forty-five minutes to get there and it was hard to get the appointment, I'd probably wait." Ask them to elaborate.

Listen to their responses. If they mention doing something while waiting or say, "I never go anywhere without bringing something to do, like having a book to read," that indicates the candidate doesn't waste time. That's a good sign. What you're looking for is whether the candidate takes initiative and places a premium on using time wisely. This is such an important insight to have about someone you may hire. After all, how many employees sit around and waste time until the boss gives them something to do? This simple exercise might help identify an applicant who uses time purposefully to their best advantage.

Interview Question 4: If I were to talk to your former boss about your performance, what are three outstanding strengths they would say you have? (Ask this question ten to fifteen minutes after Question 1. Deliberately space Questions 1 and 4 apart, asking other questions between them.)

Purpose and Value: Here you're looking for correlations between their answers to Questions 1 and 4. It has been said that *what we admire in others is oftentimes a reflection of ourselves.* The admired characteristics in others that match their own strengths give you some insight into whether there's alignment with characteristics of a Pro-Achiever. Look carefully for such alignment.

Interview Question 5: What would you do in the following situation? You and your boss are in a meeting with one of the company's top customers. Everything is going smoothly and according to plan until your boss criticizes you in front of the customer for something you definitely didn't do. At that moment, what do you do or say?

Purpose and Value: Rarely will a candidate say they would point out the boss's error in front of the customer. Most will say, "I would wait until the meeting ended before saying something to the boss." Once more, you're seeking to learn how the candidate thinks their way through certain situations that have relevance on the job. Build on the situation by addressing the following development: After the candidate says they would wait until later to say something, say, "Okay. While you're expressing your concerns, the boss is dismissing them and attributing very little importance to the incident. Now, what do you do or say?" Listen carefully to their response to see whether they're more narrowly focused on themselves or on the bigger picture in which they may mention what the boss might be dealing with at the time. By asking some additional questions, you may also gain some insights about whether the candidate is forgiving. After all, when we make a mistake in the workplace, we want our bosses to forgive us and accept the fact that we're only human. When it's the boss who has made the error, do we give them the same leniency and understanding? You're looking for whether the candidate is reasonable, thinks more broadly about situations, is forgiving, and demonstrates some flexibility. All of these are important aspects of Pro-Achievers.

Introducing These Questions: If these questions appear different from your usual set of interview questions, that's understandable! They're different from what most people consider to be a routine set of interview questions. But don't let that deter you from asking them. The fact that they're so different is what makes them effective in distinguishing average candidates from current or potential Pro-Achievers.

From the standpoint of an interviewee, most interviews are quite easy to prepare for since they're mostly routine in nature and allow for rehearsal. What makes these questions particularly efficacious is their surprise value; they require a think-on-your-feet kind of spontaneity on the part of an interviewee. And don't worry, they're legal and can't be categorized as culturally insensitive or unfair.

What you're likely wondering is how best to introduce them. A number of managers have found it effective to introduce them by simply saying, "The next few questions involve putting yourself in a variety of scenarios. I'd like you to explain how you would respond to each of them."

If time is short or it's too costly to conduct face-to-face interviews, then you might consider asking these or similar questions as part of your written test. Below are a few others that have served hiring managers well. Included beside each answer is an explanation to better understand what the question is looking for. Keep in mind that you can formulate your own questions as well. Be sure to test them out with others ahead of time to determine if they're interpreted as intended. Also, make sure the questions reflect and are relevant to the job being filled.

SAMPLE WRITTEN TEST

(To download this form go to: www.drdebbright.com/
pro-achievement-bonus-page)

Choose the action you believe to be the best way to
address each of the following situations.

1. At work you have too much to do and too little time to accomplish all your tasks within normal work hours. Nevertheless, as you examine your to-do list, you find that each item is important.
Choose **just one** of the options below that you would most likely do:

a. Jump in and do the most challenging things first. *(This is what many people have been taught, but it is the least preferred answer because doing the "toughest" task may not, in the end, yield the greatest valuable difference.)*

b. Go to your boss and ask for help. *(Seems reasonable. However, a person operating with Personal Responsibleness will take initiative to build their own priority list before seeking alignment with the boss.)*

c. Develop a priority list and then go to your boss to review it. *(This is **the preferred choice**. This person is operating with Personal Responsibleness but making sure a valuable difference is realized by coordinating with the boss.)*

d. Start going through your to-do list and stay until everything is done, even if it means working late. *(Those with Personal Responsibleness, though dependable and others-focused, know that making a valuable difference requires teamwork and coordinated effort.)*

e. Ask a coworker for help. *(This is also a **preferred choice** because those with Personal Responsibleness are problem-solvers; they seek out resources to ensure the work gets done and a valuable difference is realized.)*

Explain your answer.

2. Your boss provides you with very little feedback on how you are performing at your job. You feel as though you are always in the dark. Other people who report to the same boss agree with you. Select from the following choices how you would address the situation.

a. Go to the boss and ask plainly how you're doing. *(This is too direct and likely to make the boss uncomfortable. It is unlikely to result in a productive discussion; this approach basically asks the boss to deliver an instant performance review.)*

b. Accept that the boss is the way he is and learn to live with it. *(This is too passive a stance and could lead to a faulty conclusion that the boss is uninvolved and disinterested.)*

c. Write up your own performance assessment, then go to the boss for feedback. *(This is **the preferred response** because the individual is taking initiative to seek input. Rather than complain to others, the individual has accurately assessed the best course of action and followed through in a way that won't put the boss on the spot.)*

d. Complain to your boss's boss or go to HR for help. *(This choice may be appropriate only after other attempts have been made to resolve the issue. Selecting this route immediately is an "easy way out" and doesn't show much creativity. It also sends the message that the employee tends to self-focus.)*

e. Talk to your colleagues and seek advice for how to collectively approach the boss. *(This is not a preferred choice because, if the boss is uncomfortable providing feedback, a gang approach will do little to make the boss receptive and open to giving feedback.)*

Explain your answer.

3. Your boss always asks you to do things at the last minute, especially when it's almost time to go home. Each time this happens you end up leaving late, which creates some tension at home. Select from the following choices how you would address the situation.

  a. Complain the next time your boss gives you last-minute assignments at the end of the day. *(This demonstrates a lack of acceptance of control.)*

  b. Go to an HR representative and talk about the issue. *(While this option isn't out of the question, it demonstrates an overreaction and an unwillingness to go to the source to solve an issue.)*

  c. Set an appointment with the boss or, preferably, approach the boss at a convenient time to address the situation. *(This is **the preferred choice** because the individual is recognizing the importance of timing, unlike option A. Selecting a neutral time makes it easier for all parties involved to focus on the situation at hand. Dropping by makes the conversation less formal.)*

  d. Vent to a peer about the situation and try to get over it. *(While talking with a peer may momentarily alleviate frustration, the peer can't do anything to rectify the situation like the boss can.)*

  e. Start going to the boss midday to see if there's anything urgent that needs to be done by end of day. *(This is also a **preferred choice**, although it is less direct. It shows that the individual has assessed where their control lies and is taking an effective route to solve an issue. This approach includes the solution. Over time, you hope the boss will eventually catch on.)*

  Explain your answer.

4. A customer calls you and asks a question that doesn't fall into your particular area, so you give the customer the number for the correct department. When you casually relay this to your boss, the boss isn't pleased. Why? *(Look for the individual to reflect on the following: "If a customer is calling me, even by mistake, I know that I represent the company to that person. Therefore, it's up to me to make sure the customer is satisfied. While it may take more effort on my part, it is, indeed, in my control to see to it that the customer gets connected with the correct person."*

Explain your answer.

5. Your boss asks you to do something with which you disagree. You think that if you do what the boss asks, it will make things worse. What do you say?

    a. Say nothing and do what your boss asks. After all, this is your boss. *(Represents an attitude that doesn't promote the importance of striving to make a valuable difference.)*

    b. Go to your boss and suggest that taking this course of action may not get the results needed or desired. *(This is* **the preferred choice** *because it demonstrates sensitivity and respect for others, especially those in positions of authority.)*

    c. Tell your boss that you think the assignment is wrong and go on to explain your idea. *(The focus here is too narrow. Attention is directed to who is right or wrong.)*

    d. Ask questions of your boss to learn more about the boss's reasoning before deciding to speak up or not. *(This is another* **preferred choice** *because it represents awareness that what the boss says might be linked to some bigger picture. The individual is showing sensitivity to others, and openness to learning about the macro perspective discussed earlier.)*

    e. Don't do what the boss asked. Do what you think is best. *(Represents an attitude that doesn't promote the importance of striving to make a valuable difference.)*

    Explain your answer.

INTERPRETING CANDIDATES' RESPONSES

It can be beneficial to comparatively quantify outstanding candidates. For preferred responses, hiring managers may decide to award one or two points, depending on the importance or weight given to each situation or question asked. The weight given to each question may be based on how closely the situations align with the actual job responsibilities the candidate will be expected to perform.

Look at the total number of points for the oral questions and written test. The candidate with the greatest number of points most exemplifies a Pro-Achiever. Keep in mind that none of the questions assess the candidate's skill level. Determining whether the candidate is competent and has the proper skill set requires additional interviewing approaches.

In an atmosphere of Pro-Achievers, it's common for performance levels to be at consistently high levels and for employees to feel that they work in a trusting environment where it's actually fun to engage. When team members look forward to coming to work every day, getting up in the morning becomes that much easier.

SCORING FORM

As mentioned earlier in this lesson, you might want to create your own scoring methodology for each interview process. Here is one recording format and point system you may find convenient:

Personal Responsibleness Screening Tool
Sample: Phone/Oral Interview

(To download this form go to: www.drdebbright.com/
pro-achievement-bonus-page)

Screening Questions/Criteria	Comments	Points
1. Did you finish high school? *No – 0 pts.* *Yes – 2 pts.*		
2. After completing high school, did you go to college? If no, why not? *Award 1 pt. if candidate:* • *attended college* • *chose to attend a vocational school or an apprenticeship* • *was obligated to care for a family member or other similar circumstance* *Award 1 pt. more (for a total of 2 pts.) if candidate:* • *completed college, vocational school, or alternate commitment* • *successfully fulfilled other obligation (e.g., military) / was not self-focused* *Award 1 pt. more (for a total of 3 pts.) if candidate:* *paid their way through college/ training.*		

3. Whether at your previous job, school, or at home, identify one thing you are proud of. *Follow-up Questions:* • How did you come up with this idea? *Award 1 pt. if it was their idea.* • Did you successfully complete it? *Award 1 pt. if they did.* • Did you have to rely on others to achieve it? *Award 1 pt. if they either did not or if they credit others gracefully.* (Maximum of 3 pts.)		

Interview Questions/Criteria	Comments	Points
1. Ideal characteristics: 　　1. 　　2. 　　3. (Maximum up to 3 pts.)	Did the characteristics match?	
2. Server scenario. *Award 1 pt. for the ability to think the situation through, 1 pt. for micro thinking, 1 pt. for macro thinking.* (Maximum of 3 pts.)		
3. Doctor appointment scenario. *Award 1 pt. for the ability to think the situation through, 1 pt. for being prepared to use time well, 1 pt. for thinking about work and personal obligations.* (Maximum of 3 pts.)		
4. Public criticism scenario. *Award 1 pt. for the ability to think the situation through, 1 pt. for **not** speaking up right away, 1 pt. for being considerate of the boss.* (Maximum of 3 pts.)		
		Total:

A FINAL CONSIDERATION FOR YOUR SEARCH

If possible, include people within your own organization in your search for a replacement or additional staff opening. Keep in mind that people within most organizations rarely let it be known that they're dissatisfied with their job, boss, or those with whom they work. In fact, you won't find Pro-Achievers talking about such things, and you're looking to recruit the Pro-Achievers. Remember, true Pro-Achievers are team players and, as a matter of personal integrity, don't necessarily leap to self-serving opportunities every time they arise. Before acting on a job opportunity that becomes available in another department, Pro-Achievers typically consider how such a move would impact their current team or department, and how it would affect the goals of the boss, the team, and the organization as a whole.

To recruit a Pro-Achiever from within your organization, you'll need to take some time to carefully consider whom you're familiar with and to what degree they appear to have the characteristics of a Pro-Achiever. Once you identify one or two internal candidates, approach them and casually suggest that the two of you go out for a coffee or a bite to eat. Whether or not they know you're headhunting, don't mention the purpose of the get-together. Let them ask you at your *tête-à-tête*. You may be surprised to learn they already know your purpose and need. Even if they say nothing or don't claim awareness of your need, you might want to open the conversation with, "Do you know anyone who's worth interviewing for a position I need to fill? The reason I'm asking you before anyone else is because I respect your judgment and your work ethic." That opens the door. See if they take it from there!

LESSON 5 *Takeaway Points for Review*

- Try to get an idea whether the resume reflects a candidate who completed goals.

- Consider giving "extra credit" to candidates who paid their own way through school, served in the military, or worked for a social cause they truly believed in. Another admirable trait might be that they worked to help with family income.

- If the position requires interaction with others, such as with customers or colleagues, it's important to screen candidates for their phone presence and the ability to use proper grammar and speak clearly.

- Explore what the candidate is most proud of achieving and the difficulties that were experienced during the process. That conversation may offer insight into what the candidate considers "working hard" and whether the candidate tends to be more about self, as opposed to being interested in the broader value derived from the effort.

- Pay particular attention to whether the candidate graciously gives credit to others regarding some of their more noted accomplishments.

- Consider having the candidate e-mail an assignment to you or a colleague within a reasonable amount of time. If the assignment was handled correctly and delivered on time, then consider the quality of the write-up.

- If the position requires a high proficiency of writing skills, the hiring manager should examine the candidate's writing ability closely.

- Ask questions that indicate whether the candidate accepts control and operates with an achieving attitude.

- We strongly suggest that you use the interview questions and tests appearing in this lesson. They require a think-on-your-feet kind of spontaneity on the part of an interviewee. They are legal and in no way culturally insensitive or unfair.

- In your search for candidates, be sure to consider people within your own organization who have the characteristics of a Pro-Achiever.

~

LESSON 6

INTRODUCING THE PRO-ACHIEVEMENT PRINCIPLE TO YOUR TEAM

N ow may be the time to seriously consider bringing what you've learned about The Pro-Achievement Principle to those with whom you work, be it the entire team, your direct reports, or perhaps a few select coworkers in other departments.

With the understanding you've gained from the first five lessons of this BIZLET, you have all the fundamental knowledge and resources necessary to explain the traits of a Pro-Achiever. But influencing others to become Pro-Achievers requires more than having knowledge of the subject. To engage others to join you in this pursuit, you'll need to put on a leader's hat and be a catalyst. What is important to emphasize is that engaging others is not the equivalent of sending an order or telling people what to do. Rather, your role as a leader is to heighten their awareness as you introduce the attributes of Pro-Achieving.

IT'S TIME TO PUT ON YOUR LEADERSHIP HAT

Being an effective leader requires having in varying degrees and at different times, the talents of a teacher as well as a coach. Great coaches and teachers do less talking and more asking in order to bring out the best in others. By heightening one's awareness when introducing the "how," they inspire individuals to want to change.

This lesson begins with suggestions for how you can open these inspiring conversations about Pro-Achievement. Everyone wants to feel they're an important part of a winning team. If you think of yourself as the coach, this is your opportunity to provide them with the "how to" of achieving that desire. Only by way of their willingness to understand and practice Pro-Achievement traits will people come to realize their ambition to become a Pro-Achiever. Helping along that willingness is the key objective of your role in this lesson.

INITIATING YOUR APPROACH

STARTING A CONVERSATION ABOUT PRO-ACHIEVEMENT

While introducing others to the subject of Pro-Achievement is a matter that is up to your own style, here are some **coaching tips** for enhancing your effectiveness in sparking the interest in others.

COACHING TIP 1:
Introduce the Concept by Handing Out the Book

If your leadership style includes introducing creative ideas to your team for the purpose of stimulating thought, then coming to work one day and passing along this BIZLET to team members may be comfortable for you and extremely effective.

If you haven't used this approach in the past but would like to, you might want to provide a reason for your sudden burst of didactic generosity in passing along *The Pro-Achievement Principle.*

Perhaps handing out a copy or two might tie in with a major theme you've been promoting such as "greater collaboration," encouraging everyone to "take more initiative," or being more "customer-focused." As their leader or as a fellow team member, you can probably think of numerous appropriate matters that relate directly to the pertinence of the BIZLET's content.

COACHING TIP 2:
Become a Pro-Achievement Advocate to the Uninitiated

As an alternative to directly using the BIZLET as a catalyst, consider engaging everyone at a team meeting in a discussion about their best and worst customer experiences. When you start peeling apart the layers of each story to determine what made the greatest difference between success and failure, point out that more often than not, the individual makes the difference. Leverage this point as an opportunity to introduce the nature of the Pro-Achiever, in which the individual understands and accepts control and does whatever they can to realize a valuable difference. Emphasize that the individual chose to make the valuable difference. That's a great segue for expounding upon the concept of Pro-Achievement and eventually introducing the two attributes that make up The Pro-Achievement Principle: *responsibleness* and an *achieving attitude*.

COACHING TIP 3:
Utilize the Lesson Takeaway Points in Your Introduction

As noted previously, the Takeaway Points listed at the end of lessons are there to provide readers with a convenient way to refresh their memory, and to offer a quick lecture outline covering the core ideas of the BIZLET.

KEEP THE CONVERSATION GOING

The extent to which you know and understand your direct reports and how they'll best benefit from learning to be a Pro-Achiever will dictate how to approach them with a follow-up conversation.

The best opportunity for discussion of Pro-Achievement with members of your team may occur during meetings that focus on things such as performance within a project, relationships with others, attitude, mission, and objectives. Annual, monthly, or weekly reviews having to do with goals and objectives often permit opportunities to introduce the concept of Pro-Achieving as in, "Have you ever heard of the Principle of Pro-Achieving?"

Whether you choose to have a casual "let's have a chat" approach or bring everyone together for a more formal meeting, use your instincts toward what works best with those you consider to be your "students."

Consider the culture of your department or organization and ask yourself if it might be more appropriate to start with some of your closer, more trusted employees who seem to show outward traits of a Pro-Achiever. Engage those select few by suggesting that you'd like them to help you motivate others to operate as Pro-Achievers.

Do they think it's best to have a seminar on the topic, continue to introduce the concepts as an extra agenda item during weekly staff meetings, or promote the introduction of these essential attributes on a one-on-one basis? Perhaps it's a combination of all of these; asking this first group will begin to answer these questions while engaging them as early adopters.

COACHING TIP 4:
Consider Initiating a Small Pilot Program

Thinking of the bigger picture is important too. For example, you might want to use your select few as kind of a pilot or test case that, if successful, could be expanded to more people or passed along to other departments within the organization, including HR.

Whether you're meeting one-on-one or as a small group, take 60-90 minutes to talk about their thoughts after having read the book. You could also explore the underlying attributes that enable individuals to consistently meet or exceed customer or team expectations and add greater value.

For those not familiar with the BIZLET, at some point during your discussion (you'll know when), it will become appropriate to introduce key teaching points (based, if you like, on the lesson Takeaways) to communicate and illustrate Pro-Achievement concepts.

STICK WITH YOUR PURPOSE

Keep in mind that ***your purpose is not to turn people into Pro-Achievers; only they can do that***. Your purpose is to inspire a willingness to commit to a habit of thought in trying to make a valuable difference in what they do.

Think about this: No one asked you to make any formal commitment to practice the Principle of Pro-Achievement. You became inspired by reading this BIZLET and you came to appreciate the value in the principle and how practicing it could improve your relationship with others, lead to the achievement of your own life objectives, and increase the confidence you have in what you can and cannot control. All that was involved was simply making a commitment to yourself; always keep that commitment at the forefront of all you pursue.

BEING A PRO-ACHIEVER COMES FROM ONE'S OWN DETERMINATION.

After discussing the subject or giving others some time to read the BIZLET, allow them time to think it through and figure out on their own how they can employ the practice of Pro-Achieving in the way they handle matters both big and small. Give them a week or two (or longer) to let ideas marinate. You want your team or coworkers to view this not as an assignment, but as a lasting endeavor to bring about positive and meaningful changes to their lives and work habits. You may want to have subsequent meetings with them to talk over some finer points of being a Pro-Achiever. Make sure they fully understand that they play the central role in accepting the decision to practice the Principle of Pro-Achievement.

COACHING TIP 5: Reinforce the Basics with Your Pilot Team

Once the select few have some exposure to either your discussion or to the BIZLET itself, consider asking each of them (at a follow-up meeting) to provide a definition of what they understand the Principle of Pro-Achievement to be. Pick out the best definition given and ask others to raise their hand to indicate their agreement or disagreement with what is said. Soon a discussion will begin. Listen and look closely into what each person says. Listen for a definition that includes the mention of **acceptance of control** for what people think, say, and do. Also, approve no definition unless it includes the word **commitment** as in, "It's about a commitment to making things better in big as well as small ways." Someone might well offer the ideal definition that goes something like, "It's about making a personal commitment to uphold and to utilize the control one has over things to the best of one's ability. It uses two attributes, **responsibleness** and an **achieving attitude,** as a way of propelling one's actions in a positive forward direction where adding value is foremost on one's mind throughout the day." Now, anyone who says that last definition gets a day off! But you know what? The person may not take it because true Pro-Achievers routinely go beyond what's normally requested of them without expecting a reward.

MAKING IT ABOUT OTHERS

Once it becomes apparent that you're gaining at least a willingness (if not an all-out demonstrable pledge) from a few to take on the acceptance of Pro-Achievement, you've made great progress. While it may not exactly be a "commitment," at least you've gotten some people who want to give practicing Pro-Achievement a try. Congratulations, that's quite an accomplishment!

Now you can start looking for examples of where people are trying to do things better than what's normally expected. These could be things as seemingly small as signs of politeness such as an increase in how often you hear "thank you" each day. Or there might be a noticeable increase in outward cooperation with one another on the teams and in your department. Maybe you'll overhear more people saying things like, "Would you mind if I give you a better idea for handling the XYZ matter?"

A few startling things you'll begin to notice once people start putting Pro-Achieving into practice is an uptick in overall morale, a marked improvement in cooperation with one another, and an increase in suggestions for improving things, to name just a few.

Also, don't be hesitant about challenging people when you see what they could do better, or where they could add greater value, when discussing various everyday situations. They won't take what you say as criticism as maybe they would have before. Instead, they'll take suggestions as keeping with the spirit of the Pro-Achieving atmosphere you're trying to foster.

Likewise, in meetings, look for examples of where individuals Pro-Achieved and make it a point to credit those achievements publicly. Think of your credits as small rewards, and your people will too.

THINGS TO WATCH OUT FOR

Don't get discouraged if most people who've been introduced to the Principle of Pro-Achievement don't immediately become proponents. While gaining an understanding of the Principle isn't difficult, people don't change so easily. Some won't immediately get it and will need to see it working for others, especially others they admire and respect, before they decide to buy in. Focus on your select few and, eventually, curiosity will take hold and word will start to spread like a fashion trend. Be ready for questions that come from people you never imagined would show interest!

DEFENSIVENESS

Where you sense an opportunity to discuss a better way of doing things or adding value, watch out for people who might misinterpret your intentions and comments to imply that they were doing something wrong. It's important to remind them that they can go from good to better, or from better to best. It's not in any way about being wrong or inadequate. It's about getting used to thinking how things can, perhaps, be done better.

SLOW LEARNERS

Be aware of those who take one step forward and two steps back. Take care to encourage them personally. They can be of immense value to the organization once they catch on and feel part of the new atmosphere

PRO-ACHIEVEMENT PRINCIPLE

where making a valuable difference is the code word and its own reward.

REINFORCING PROPONENTS

In time, word will spread, and people will begin asking questions about what this "Pro-Achieving thing" is all about. Interest might come from HR, upper management, other departments, or from other teams. This curiosity should be taken as a signal that perhaps the time has come to broaden the base of those informed about the Principle of Pro-Achievement.

Introducing the concept to a growing population of interested people in your organization is a perfect opportunity to begin periodic sessions where a discussion on doing things better is the focus. Such sessions would reinforce the commitment to Pro-Achieving among the existing proponents and, at the same time, inspire others to consider the benefits of adopting the principle themselves. These sessions could include answering questions about broader subjects such as the traits involved in The Pro-Achievement Principle. Or, sessions could take on questions and ideas concerning the how, why, what, and who regarding implementation of ideas for doing things better.

ANTICIPATED QUESTIONS

The following are some questions you can expect about what The Principle of Pro-Achievement is and how it might best be implemented.

Q. *It sounds like Pro-Achieving is about making a valuable difference in everything someone does. Isn't that asking a lot? Why not just have people start with a goal or two and track them on those goals?*

A. This is a great question that provides an opportunity to clear up a lot of what is misunderstood about the Principle of Pro-Achieving. (Note: This question could indicate a person who views the employment and management of the principle as coming from someone outside their personal control such as a boss, team leader, or trainer/supervisor, i.e., that someone is monitoring or "tracking" the progress they're making with their goals.)

The Principle is, in fact, completely initiated and committed to by the individual. Interestingly, how one views the adoption of the Principle can start with focusing on a few things that one engages in throughout their day and thinks about what could be done a little bit better than is expected to add value. It could be something as simple as making an effort to break a habit: nail-biting, overusing the word "like" in sentences, sitting with poor posture, or interrupting others in the middle of sentences.

Ironically, Pro-Achieving is not about setting goals. It's more about the "how" as opposed to thinking about achieving a particular goal that, once reached, is no longer on someone's radar. Pro-Achieving is broader than a straight-line method or activity for the accomplishment of a specific goal. Instead, it is a self-discipline involving a constant sense of awareness in whether one has or doesn't have control over doing things better—not perfectly, mind you, but better.

Q. *How long does it take to become a Pro-Achiever?*
A. No longer than the time it takes to understand and begin practicing the true meaning of personal responsibleness and the achieving attitude. If you embrace the attributes of Pro-Achievement, you never really stop becoming a Pro-Achiever because you are always looking for ways to challenge yourself to do, say, or think of where, how, when, and with whom to add meaningful value both big and small. It becomes your natural way of being. Pro-Achievers never are concerned about getting caught up in the status quo. If you keep up with our rapidly changing times and the influx of key technologies, this way of thinking keeps you learning and on the edge of what is happening.

You will never fall behind or become out of sync with the times.

Q. *Will I be measured or evaluated for how I operate with Pro-Achievement traits in my annual review?*
A. No. Pro-Achievement is a state of mind. What soon becomes apparent to observers of those practicing Pro-Achievement is a noticeable increase in positive results in what they undertake and their politeness and thoughtfulness when dealing with others. It's up to those practicing Pro-Achievement traits whether they want to discuss the subject with their boss, team, or as an addendum to their performance reviews.

Q. *If I don't wish to attend meetings or even participate in discussions about The Principle of Pro-Achievement, will it in any way affect how I'm viewed for advancement or my job in general?*
A. No. Practicing or adopting the Principle of Pro-Achievement is a personal matter that one decides to do on their own. It works wonderfully if a team or group of associates agree to take it on. But no one should consider it some kind of litmus test or uncooperative act if the timing or idea doesn't fit an individual's space at any given time.

Q. *If I decide to start practicing the tenets described in The Pro-Achievement Principle, but I want to practice them privately and without anyone else's knowledge, is there a support website where I can register?*

A. Indeed! You can register anonymously at http://www.drdebbright.com where you'll find answers to your questions and can read about how others work with Pro-Achievement. Also, you'll find current and relevant blogs and articles, and many other supportive suggestions from Dr. Deb Bright.

Q. *I've heard that at some point in learning about The Pro-Achievement Principle, people are encouraged to come up with a motto that can serve as a big-picture compass for the purpose and direction of how they wish to be viewed by others. Since I'm new to all this, I haven't come up with a personal motto yet. What might I temporarily use as an interim motto to get me started?*

A. Try reading Lesson 2 in the BIZLET—Responsibleness: A Core Component of Personal Achievement. At the end of that lesson, you'll be better equipped to decide for yourself what motto best fits the nature of your own ambition. In the meantime, a more global motto that explains the purposeful objective of the principle is:

"If it's to be, then count on me."

LESSON 6 *Takeaway Points for Review*

- The best opportunity for discussion of Pro-Achievement with members of your team may occur during meetings that focus on performance within a project, relationship with others, attitude, mission and objectives, etc.

- Remember, your purpose is to inspire a willingness to commit to a habit of thought, namely, in trying to make a valuable difference in what they do. Allow team members time to figure out on their own how they can employ the practice of Pro-Achieving.

- As people start putting Pro-Achieving into practice, you'll notice an uptick in overall morale, a marked improvement in cooperation with one another, and an increase in suggestions for improving things, to name just a few.

- Look for examples of where individuals Pro-Achieved and make it a point to credit those achievements publicly.

- To get started, don't confuse goal setting with finding ways consistently to meet and slightly exceed expectations and /or to create value.

~

Use the PERSONAL RESPONSIBLENESS INVENTORY FOUND ON PAGE 18 FOR EVALUATING CANDIDATES.

To print out go to:
www.drdebbright.com/pro-achievement-bonus-page

Print out and use this screening tool to evaluate and get a sense of the degree a job candidate operates with the basic tenet of Personal Responsibleness. The insights you get from the candidates' responses are a measure of what you can expect when hired.

LESSON 7
PRO-ACHIEVEMENT IN ACTION: A MODEL FOR TEAM PERFORMANCE

Think of your team as a group of musicians in an orchestra and yourself as their conductor. You would want everyone to be proficient with their individual instruments and to have a good understanding of the part they play. As the conductor, you're expected to learn entire scores and cue the musicians to enter or leave their parts at the right moment and on the right note.

Much like the orchestra conductor, you're the catalyst for coordinating the talent under your control and developing the schemes for the smooth performance of your programs as they unfold. But you have no baton to wave to begin the action of the scheduled performance and carry it to a successful result. Don't you wish it were that easy? You must rely on your team members to decide when, where, and how they use their control in accomplishing their responsibilities.

By now, you know a lot about how Pro-Achievers make a big difference in getting desired results for themselves, teams, or other groups. You have a good idea of what to look for when hiring Pro-Achievers and how to help others to acquire Pro-Achieving traits and eventual habits that can move anticipated results from good to better and from better to best. Try to imagine what an entire team of Pro-Achievers operating together looks like in action.

Let's look at how Ana, a senior level manager who heads up a compliance group for a large NYC financial institution, introduced the concept of Pro-Achievement in the workplace to her employees. During the previous month, she and a few of her reports had been reading and discussing the merits of The Pro-Achievement Principle. Ana felt that since the department was entering a very busy period filled with a slew of regulatory deadlines and financial reporting requirements, it wouldn't hurt to familiarize the broader organization with what a workplace could accomplish if most workers tried to practice what Pro-Achievement is all about.

A contributing factor to Ana's decision was her increasing awareness of how many team members seemed disturbingly quick to make routine excuses, blame others for what were really shared failures, and offer weak justifications for why work wasn't completed on time.

At the beginning of the monthly departmental meeting, Ana set the stage by introducing a scenario of a typical workday involving various team members who work in a regulated area. She asked everyone in the room to carefully read the scenario and discuss with one another what the team in the scenario did well. The following is an accurate representation of her handout:

SCENARIO: ACTION MODEL FOR THE WORKPLACE

Meet Jay, an accountant at Darling Jones Company located in the Midwest. The company manufactures airplane parts, has been in business for almost twenty years, and has about 1,000 employees. Jay has worked there for about three years and he reports directly to Alicia, the financial director. One Monday morning while walking to his cubicle, Jay is greeted right away by Alicia. She very often works over the weekend and comes in fresh on Monday morning with several immediate tasks for Jay to complete. Before he gets to sit down at his desk, Alicia approaches him and, with a sense of urgency, rattles off what she needs him to do. She tells him she needs the financial report he's been working on to include some new data and that it's now due by the end of the week. Before heading back to her office, Alicia asks Jay if he anticipates any issues or if he needs any additional support, given the short timeline. Jay assures Alicia that he thinks he can get everything done in time.

Feeling the urgency of the task before him, Jay is off and running. It quickly dawns on Jay that the new information he needs must come from his coworker, Cathy. After calling and leaving a voice message, he texts her to let her know it's urgent. Cathy responds promptly to his text message, and the two of them agree that she'll get him the financials needed within the next couple of days.

On Wednesday, Cathy is working diligently to get everything done when she receives a special request from the legal department that she must address. It's urgent and cannot be ignored. Now, Cathy has a predicament. Rather than panic, she thinks the situation through and decides to reach out to a colleague of hers, Dan, to ask for some help. Unfortunately, Dan's calendar is full, and he can't do what Cathy needs within her timeframe. Rather than dismissing the request with a quick apology, Dan figures out that Susan could help. She's relatively new to the department, yet when speaking with Susan, Dan learns that she is very knowledgeable about financial reporting. Instead of emailing Susan's contact information to Cathy, Dan reasons that, since Cathy doesn't know Susan well and given the tight turnaround time on this project, he'd best walk Cathy over to Susan's office and introduce them.

Before meeting with Susan, Cathy makes a quick detour to give Jay a heads-up that she's running into a few setbacks and asks if she can have a little more time to get him the information he requested. Jay is fine with that request. Feeling somewhat relieved, Cathy quickly reunites with Dan as they continue on their way to Susan's office to explain the urgency of the situation.

As Susan is listening to what Cathy is requesting, she politely interrupts because an idea pops into her mind. She shares with Cathy a suggestion for how they could more efficiently pull together some information and, at the same time, get another set of data that would present an even more complete picture. Cathy is delighted. She confesses to Susan that, for the past year, no one has suggested how to use some of the newer programs to extract data more easily. "Your timing with this idea couldn't have been better," she praises Susan.

Susan agrees to help her out, and they decide together that Susan will send everything over to Cathy by 9:00 the next morning. Cathy thanks Dan for introducing her to Susan. "No problem," says Dan. "I didn't want to put you in an awkward position. You already have a tight deadline to worry about."

Soon after, Cathy gets back to Jay and updates him. He's already made an adjustment in his calendar to accommodate Cathy's need for another day. Cathy decides to stay late to work as much as she can on Jay's project so she can devote the next morning to completing the urgent request from legal.

The next day, Susan delivers what she promised to Cathy. As Cathy reviews what Susan completed, she's now positioned to put all the puzzle pieces together to get everything to Jay by the end of the day, as agreed. In the end, Jay is able to hand everything to Alicia as promised on Friday morning.

FOLLOWING THIS...

Ana, while standing in the front of the conference room, took a deep breath, then paused and asked the assembled group, "What did this team do well?"

At first, they were quiet. Then, Joey, one of the more senior members on Ana's team, shared that what impressed him was how willing Dan was to make Cathy's problem his own problem. The group nodded in agreement. Another member, Asha, pointed out that it was wise and thoughtful of Dan to take the time to introduce Cathy to Susan. She added that it would have been easy to simply tell Cathy to reach out to Susan on her own. Others chimed in, pointing out how Cathy was also determined to do whatever she could to get the task done for Jay. She kept her word. Rather than throw the problem back at Jay, she sought out solutions, and even stayed late to ensure everything got done. Others in the meeting commented on how great it was for Cathy to keep Jay in the loop by notifying him promptly about how things were going so Jay could adjust his schedule. Others pointed out that Jay was also accommodating. He offered to help Cathy get everything done. Another team member pointed out how impressive it was that Susan came up with a better idea instead of simply doing what was asked of her, and this team member was also impressed at how Cathy was so receptive to Susan's idea, even though she hadn't thought of it herself.

Ana wrote all these thoughts on a white board as she heard them. When she felt she'd accurately captured everyone's input, she began to refer to their statements and elaborate on them.

"Let's peel these back like an onion and examine what's underlying their actions." Ana went on to say, "There are two attributes layered on top of each other, clearly connected, that help to explain the actions of these individuals. Keep in mind, no boss was present throughout the scenario. No one was telling them what to do. Each member took it upon themselves to do whatever was necessary or within their control to move things forward." Ana gestured to the white board while saying, "Taking other people's problems and making them your own. Being a problem solver and setting one's own standards, as Susan did. Being willing to break from the norm and offer new ideas in an effort to improve things. Keeping your word . . . all these actions are indicative of someone who exemplifies personal responsibleness and an achieving attitude."

Then Ana proceeded to go deeper into describing to all The Principle of Pro-Achievement as something each person in the room could adopt. She took the time to reinforce the difference between responsibilities and responsibleness. She cited how with personal responsibilities, we either take them on or are given them by others such as our boss, peers, mates, parents, or even society, and that they are externally driven. Personal responsibleness, on the other hand, comes into a person's nature by way of their own will and self-discipline. She continued to explain that personal responsibleness comes from one's willingness to accept the control they have in making a valuable difference. She noted that it was the chief characteristic of those in the scenario.

Ana asked her team members to consider what they would like to do to ensure, as a team, they do things a bit better and strive to make a valuable difference.

PRO-ACHIEVEMENT: PUTTING IT INTO ACTION

Think of an engaging way to introduce the ideas of personal responsibleness and an achieving attitude to your employees in an appropriate way for them and your organization's culture. If not taking Ana's approach, you might consider asking them to examine what attributes and behaviors are characteristic of those who consistently deliver excellent customer experiences. When you point out how these individuals do what's in their control to service customers, you're priming your people to think and talk about personal responsibleness and an achieving attitude.

Don't hesitate to bring out the word Pro-Achievement and point out that Pro-Achievers have some not-so-obvious attributes, such as always keeping in mind the interests of others. When asked to do something, they try to ensure they understand the directive and then deliver at a level that matches or exceeds expectations. They are always looking to make a valuable difference and distinguish themselves by use of willpower and all the resources they possess.

To help everyone integrate this way of thinking and operating, start a conversation to explore what they believe is needed to function more effectively as a team. When doing this, keep in mind that the ideas and recommendations need to come from them, as opposed to your introducing some type of directive. That's what Ana did. Here's how she facilitated her meeting:

Ana asked the team to collectively come up with what they agree to think and do starting the next day, as a way to harmonize team efforts. She reminded everyone of the importance of functioning more effectively together as a team, given the forthcoming high-peak work demands, including all the regulatory requirements needing to be met.

You'll be surprised how welcoming your people will be to what Ana's team agreed to, namely:

- Make other people's problems your own.

- Keep agreements; don't say yes to a timeline as a way of being agreeable.

- Don't be quick to blame others for failures you could have helped prevent.

Let your people cooperate in listing rules that make sense to them—and you. Once they begin these discussions, you'll feel the energy within the group begin to build up. Let it do so!

Try building off the excitement generated in the room with the following: "What happens if one of you doesn't follow or uphold these rules we're establishing? As you know, these aren't things we've been doing consistently, and, if we're being realistic, we need to come up with a plan in case someone doesn't uphold their commitments."

Be sure to write down suggestions as they occur. Study the receptivity to suggestions as you look around the room. Have the group clarify anything that appears confusing or complicated.

Without seeming too forceful, interject some of your own ideas. For instance, you may want to suggest they consider agreeing to solve problems at the lowest level possible. You might add, "If you escalate the situation to me, the first thing I'm going to ask is, 'Have you talked to the person directly to try to resolve the issue?' I won't go any further until you've tried to do so."

Suggest a "trial week," in which everyone has the opportunity to practice implementing the attributes of Pro-Achieving and upholding the newly endorsed rules of etiquette, as well as how best to approach one another. To end the session, share with the group your own enthusiasm toward their creative thinking and ambitions to develop a better place for all to work. Throw in a motivational quote such as the inspiring message from John Wooden, one of college basketball's most revered coaches:

DON'T MEASURE YOURSELF BY WHAT YOU HAVE ACCOMPLISHED, BUT BY WHAT YOU SHOULD HAVE ACCOMPLISHED WITH YOUR ABILITY.
JOHN WOODEN

SUMMARY OF ACTION STEPS

- Create for your team a detailed picture of what an achieving environment looks like or ask your team to recall occasions when they were involved in such an environment. Alternatively, have them imagine what an achieving environment would look like in a team setting. Be sure that specifics are mentioned during the exchange.

- Ask the team to develop, as opposed to you providing the insights, what's needed for the team to do better when interacting with one another.

- Facilitate the discussion by making sure that expectations are clearly established and can be easily spotted by all team members.

- Recommend a one-week "trial run" to give everyone on the team some time to develop the habit of exercising control so they're more effective. After all, the desire may be there but turning these behaviors into habits may, and most likely will, take some time.

FINAL THOUGHTS

The alchemic transformation to Pro-Achieving is one that occurs in conjunction with discovery and awareness. This isn't a simple pursuit. It requires one's effort throughout the day to spot opportunities where one can add value or do things a little bit better. Over time, Pro-Achieving becomes part of one's being. If we stopped trying, it would mean we had reached perfection, whether as an individual or as a team. No one and no team is perfect. Striving to make a valuable difference and to do things a little bit better is what results in a greater sense of personal and team satisfaction, and an enhanced level of performance that knows no limits.

END OF BIZLET

~

For additional tips and ideas on initiating interest and insights for using *The Pro-Achievement Principle* in the workplace, go to www.drdebbright.com and click to subscribe to the *Pro-Achievement Way*, a monthly coaching e-letter that will keep you and your team focused on pro-achieving throughout the year.

Printed in the USA
CPSIA information can be obtained
at www.ICGtesting.com
LVHW010014100923
757267LV00010B/957